T0015353

Field Guide to

North American Flycatchers

Field Guide to

North American Flycatchers

Kingbirds and Myiarchus

Cin-Ty Lee
Illustrated by Andrew Birch

Princeton University Press
Princeton and Oxford

Published by Princeton University Press
41 William Street, Princeton, New Jersey 08540
99 Banbury Road, Oxford OX2 6JX

press.princeton.edu

All Rights Reserved
ISBN (pbk.) 9780691240640
ISBN (e-book) 9780691244334

British Library Cataloging-in-Publication Data is available

Editorial: Robert Kirk and Megan Mendonça
Production Editorial: Mark Bellis
Cover Design: Wanda España
Production: Steve Sears
Publicity: William Pagdatoon and Caitlyn Robson
Copyeditor: Frances Cooper

Cover Credit: Andrew Birch

This book has been composed in Minion Pro (body) and Ariana Pro (headings)

Printed on acid-free paper. ∞

Typeset and designed by D & N Publishing, Wiltshire, UK

Printed in China

10 9 8 7 6 5 4 3 2 1

Contents

Kingbirds (*Tyrannus*) 101

The "yellow-bellied" Kingbirds 111

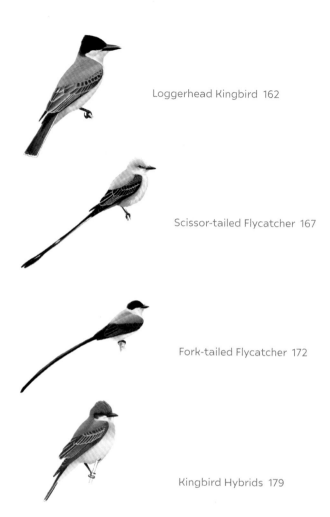

Preface

Flycatchers are often thought of as dull, nonmusical birds, sometimes impossible to identify. But for us it is different: we are drawn to their soft tones, the subtleties in their forms, and their emphatic, staccato vocals. We have spent the last couple of decades searching for and studying flycatchers in the field. In 2020, the year that Covid-19 impacted the world, we decided it was time to put our thoughts down on paper. The original goal was to publish one large tome on flycatchers, but we decided that the identification approaches for different flycatcher groups, although similar, were sufficiently different as to warrant separate treatments. Volume 1 focused on the *Empidonax* flycatchers and *Contopus* pewees. This volume focuses on the *Tyrannus* kingbirds and *Myiarchus* flycatchers. The kingbirds and *Myiarchus* are much more colorful (for a flycatcher) than *Empidonax* and pewees. Some species are unmistakable, but many of the kingbirds and all of the *Myiarchus* flycatchers still present identification challenges.

Can flycatcher identification be made a little more accessible to all, including beginners? We believe it is possible, but unlike many other birds, flycatchers can rarely be identified by a single field mark. Any given field mark for a flycatcher is slightly variable, often overlapping with those of other species. Differences between species are subtle such that two different people may very well interpret the same feature in different ways. One person's long tail, for example, might be someone else's short tail.

Despite the non-uniqueness of many field marks in flycatchers, we show here that the combination of these variable field marks is unique to a species. In this book series, our goal is to introduce holistic birding, in which identification incorporates a bird's overall appearance, behavior, vocalizations, habitat preference, and even time of year. This book trains the observer to quantify subtle differences more objectively, in shapes, color contrasts, and vocalizations. In so doing, we want to develop a common language for describing these subtle field marks.

Just as in Volume 1, this volume consists of illustrations, spectrograms, and maps; but there are no photographs. Subtle differences in color contrast are difficult to reproduce consistently in photographs due to lighting and camera exposure conditions. Only through illustrations can these subtle differences in color and shape be idealized and communicated. These two volumes serve as an introduction to the basics of flycatcher identification. One can then turn to the ever-growing online archives of photographs to test and apply your skills at your leisure. Photographs will be included in a third volume, currently in progress.

We have benefited from many colleagues in the birding and ornithological communities. We continue to be inspired by the works of Kenn Kaufman. His *Guide to Advanced Birding* was pioneering in introducing gestalt birding to the community. His *Field Guide to Birds of North America* is an example of simplifying bird identification for the masses. And, of course, we devoured his early *Birding* articles on the field identification of *Empidonax*. Donna Dittmann and Steve Cardiff's work on *Myiarchus* flycatchers provided a trove of information. Peter Pyle's identification guides were a valuable resource. We were also inspired by the illustrations of David Sibley, Lars Jonsson, and many others, whose greatest contributions, among many, have been to convey gestalt through their illustrations. The beautifully illustrated Japanese field guides by Osao and Michiaki Ujihara are truly inspirational. There are so many other exceptionally talented artists that it seems offensive to only name a few, but the works of Jen Brumfield, James Coe, Federico Gemma, Catherine Hamilton, Hans Larsson, Ian Lewington, Brian J. Small, Darren Woodhead, and Julie Zickefoose were often referenced for inspiration in creating our illustrations. The importance of distribution and migration timing was instilled in us early by Jonathan Dunn, Kimball Garrett, and Paul Lehman. Our obsession over maps goes back to the late geologist and southern California birder Doug Morton.

We are also indebted to the eBird team at the Cornell Lab of Ornithology as well as the thousands of birders who contribute data to eBird so that the timing and movements of birds are now better known than ever before. We thank the countless birders who have contributed audio recordings to xeno-canto. We have relied heavily on Richard Webster's meticulous documentation of flycatcher calls. This work could not have been accomplished without the troves of photos in the Macaulay Library and those held by Surfbirds.com.

Our journey with flycatchers has benefited from the expertise of many: Eugene and Steve Cardiff, Donna Dittmann, Ted Eubanks, the late Ned K. Johnson, Raymond Paynter, and Ron Weeks. For access to museum specimens over the years, we thank Carla Cicero for UC Berkeley, Gary Voelker and Heather Prestridge for Texas A&M University, Allison Shultz and Young Ha Suh for the Los Angeles County Natural History Museum, and Nicholas Mason, Steve Cardiff, and Donna Dittmann for Lousiana State University. Our work benefited from many eyes, including those of Jonathan Dunn, Alvaro Jaramillo, Kimball Garrett, Oscar Johnson, Tom Johnson (who sadly passed away before publication), James van Remsen, Tom Stephenson, and Ron Weeks. Oscar's deep knowledge, from taxonomy to distribution to bird identification, has been extremely helpful. Any mistakes, of course, are our own.

Finally, we could not have done this without the support of our respective families (Yu-Ye, Heru, Tiffany, Chloe, and Henry), which has allowed us to pursue our obsessions.

CIN-TY LEE, RICE UNIVERSITY, TX
ANDREW BIRCH, LOS ANGELES, CA
JULY 2023

INTRODUCTION

Flycatcher plumage and structural differences are subtle, so no single field mark can be used alone for identification. Field identification of flycatchers, however, is still possible using a combination of field marks, vocalizations, and habitat preferences. In this book, we show the reader how to see subtle differences in plumage or structural features, how to distinguish between different calls, and how to pay attention to subtleties in habitat preference. We also introduce maps with detailed information on geographic distribution and migration timing.

What are *Myiarchus* and *Tyrannus*?

The tyrant flycatcher family *Tyrannidae* is one of the largest bird families in the world with 101 genera and more than 400 species. Tyrant flycatchers are only found in the Americas, with the majority occurring in Central and tropical South America. They are mostly carnivorous, but sometimes frugivorous, catching their prey (insects and small reptiles) directly from the air, gleaning it from vegetation, or pouncing on it on the ground or other substrate. Here, we focus on a subset of the family, the genera *Myiarchus* and *Tyrannus*. These two genera consist of medium to large flycatchers—distinctly larger and slightly more colorful than the *Empidonax* flycatchers. Worldwide, there are 22 species currently recognized in the genus *Myiarchus*, with six recorded in the United States. There are 13 currently recognized species in *Tyrannus,* with ten recorded in the United States. The number of species, however, may increase in the future if some of the tropical subspecies become elevated to species status.

The typical *Myiarchus* flycatcher has gray-brown upperparts, a yellowish belly, and a long tail with variable amounts of rufous coloration. Members of *Tyrannus* are called kingbirds because of their aggressive behaviors when on territory. Fork-tailed and Scissor-tailed Flycatchers also fall into this genus: they are kingbirds with long tails. For the purposes of this guide, the kingbirds can be visually categorized into a "yellow-bellied" group and a "white-bellied" group.

The diagrams in the next few pages present an approximate model for the phylogenetic evolution of the flycatcher genera that occur in the United States and Canada (Harvey et al., 2020). *Myiarchus* and *Tyrannus*, along with the kiskadees (*Pitangus*) and the Sulphur-bellied Flycatcher (*Myiodynastes luteiventris*), evolved in a separate lineage from *Empidonax* flycatchers, pewees (*Contopus*), and phoebes (*Sayornis*). Both *Myiarchus* and *Tyrannus* originated earlier than *Empidonax*.

We also show the phylogenetic relationships of all species within the *Myiarchus* and *Tyrannus* genera, highlighting in red the ones treated in this book. Of the six *Myiarchus* flycatchers within our region, the most closely related are Ash-throated, Nutting's, Brown-crested, and Great Crested, which are also the most similar in terms of plumage and structure. La Sagra's derives from this lineage but diverged more recently. Dusky-capped separated from the Ash-throated lineage earlier and is our most unique *Myiarchus*.

The kingbird phylogeny is particularly interesting because visual similarity does not always predict genetic proximity. For example, of all the kingbirds, Western Kingbird and Scissor-tailed Flycatcher are the most closely related, but one has a short tail and the other a long tail. Tropical and Gray Kingbirds are closely related despite very different plumage colors. Tropical and Couch's Kingbirds look almost identical but are not closely related. Nevertheless, inspection of this guide will reveal that closely related kingbirds do share common body structures, habits, and vocalizations.

TYRANNIDAE PHYLOGENY

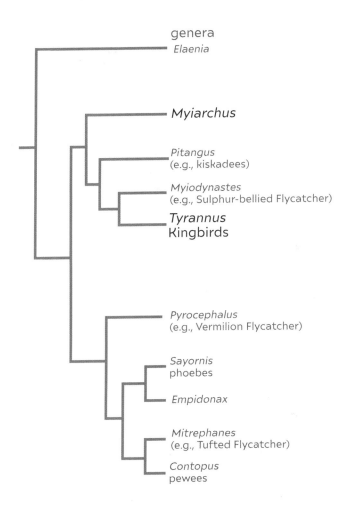

genera

Elaenia

Myiarchus

Pitangus
(e.g., kiskadees)

Myiodynastes
(e.g., Sulphur-bellied Flycatcher)

Tyrannus
Kingbirds

Pyrocephalus
(e.g., Vermilion Flycatcher)

Sayornis
phoebes

Empidonax

Mitrephanes
(e.g., Tufted Flycatcher)

Contopus
pewees

MYIARCHUS PHYLOGENY

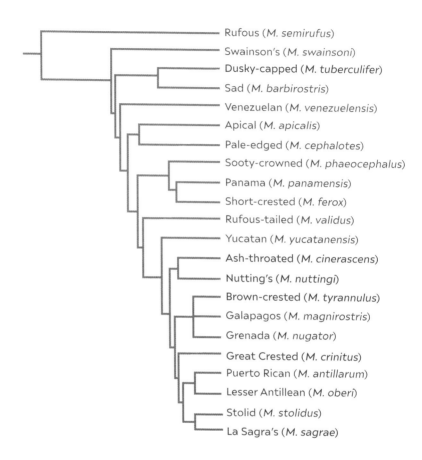

Rufous (*M. semirufus*)
Swainson's (*M. swainsoni*)
Dusky-capped (*M. tuberculifer*)
Sad (*M. barbirostris*)
Venezuelan (*M. venezuelensis*)
Apical (*M. apicalis*)
Pale-edged (*M. cephalotes*)
Sooty-crowned (*M. phaeocephalus*)
Panama (*M. panamensis*)
Short-crested (*M. ferox*)
Rufous-tailed (*M. validus*)
Yucatan (*M. yucatanensis*)
Ash-throated (*M. cinerascens*)
Nutting's (*M. nuttingi*)
Brown-crested (*M. tyrannulus*)
Galapagos (*M. magnirostris*)
Grenada (*M. nugator*)
Great Crested (*M. crinitus*)
Puerto Rican (*M. antillarum*)
Lesser Antillean (*M. oberi*)
Stolid (*M. stolidus*)
La Sagra's (*M. sagrae*)

TYRANNUS (KINGBIRD) PHYLOGENY

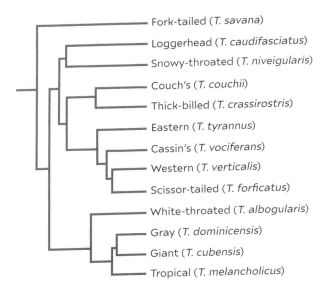

Fork-tailed (*T. savana*)

Loggerhead (*T. caudifasciatus*)

Snowy-throated (*T. niveigularis*)

Couch's (*T. couchii*)

Thick-billed (*T. crassirostris*)

Eastern (*T. tyrannus*)

Cassin's (*T. vociferans*)

Western (*T. verticalis*)

Scissor-tailed (*T. forficatus*)

White-throated (*T. albogularis*)

Gray (*T. dominicensis*)

Giant (*T. cubensis*)

Tropical (*T. melancholicus*)

TOPOLOGY OF A FLYCATCHER

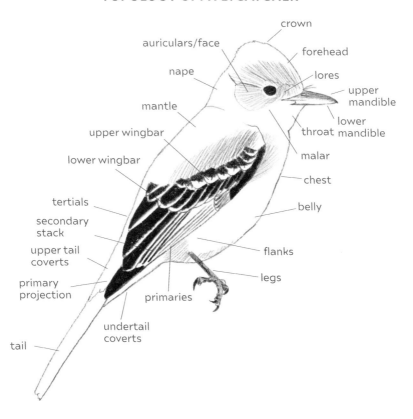

crown

auriculars/face

forehead

nape

lores

upper mandible

mantle

lower mandible

upper wingbar

throat

lower wingbar

malar

chest

tertials

belly

secondary stack

upper tail coverts

flanks

primary projection

legs

primaries

undertail coverts

tail

HOW TO USE THIS GUIDE

This guide is divided into species accounts, but before delving into these sections, we recommend viewing the identification tips discussed here. Identifying a *Myiarchus* flycatcher or *Tyrannus* kingbird requires a holistic approach using a combination of plumage and structural field marks, vocalizations, behavior, habitat preference, and seasonal timing. We explain which field marks are important and how to visualize them. We also explain how to discern the differences between vocalizations and how to use distribution and migration timing maps as aids for identification.

Bird Topology and Feather Structure

The field marks of most flycatchers are subtle and variable. The first step is to familiarize yourself with terminology associated with the topology and structure of a bird. Important areas of the bird to focus on are the **bill**, **crown**, **face**, **upperparts** (**mantle** or back), **underparts** (belly to throat), **wings** (**primaries**, **secondaries**, and **greater** and **median coverts**), and **tail**. The medium and greater coverts, when pale edged, are referred to here as the **upper** and **lower wingbars**.

The flight feathers are composed of the secondary and primary feathers, the latter forming the outer flight feathers, and the former the inner flight feathers, as seen on the following diagram (page 13) of an open wing. There are ten primaries and nine secondaries. The primary feathers are referred to with an outward numbering scheme: p1 refers to the innermost and p10 the outermost primary feather. The secondary feathers follow an inward numbering scheme: s1 is the outermost secondary and s9 is the innermost secondary. The three innermost secondaries (s7 to s9) are referred to as the **tertials**.

On the folded wing, the secondaries are referred to as the **secondary stack** or **secondary wing panel** and the primaries as the **primary stack** or **primary wing panel**. The **tertials** form the uppermost part of the secondary stack on a folded wing. In *Myiarchus*, pale edges to tertials can be conspicuous on a folded wing.

There are 12 tail feathers (**rectrices**), numbered r1 to r6 symmetrically from the center of the tail outward. The **central tail feathers** are represented by r1 to r3 and the **outer-tail feathers** represented by r4 to r6.

In some cases, understanding the structure of an individual feather is useful when studying feather color patterns. Key parts of the feather are the **shaft** (**rachis**) and the feather vanes on the outside and the inside of the shaft (distal to the body): the **outer web** and the **inner web**, respectively. For both flight and tail feathers, the width of the outer web is narrower than the inner web. The outer primaries of kingbirds are often **notched** on the inner web, especially in males. This gives the outer primary feathers in some kingbirds a highly **attenuated** appearance. Notching is not seen in *Myiarchus*, but the outer web of *Myiarchus* primaries often pinches out completely toward the tip, a feature termed as **emargination**.

TAIL FROM BELOW (*Myiarchus* tail)

closed tail

rectrix 6 = r6 outermost tail feather

r6 r5 r4 r3 r2 r1

open tail

FOLDED WING

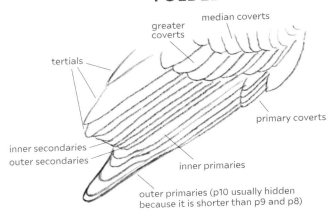

greater coverts
median coverts
tertials
inner secondaries
outer secondaries
primary coverts
inner primaries
outer primaries (p10 usually hidden because it is shorter than p9 and p8)

OPEN WING

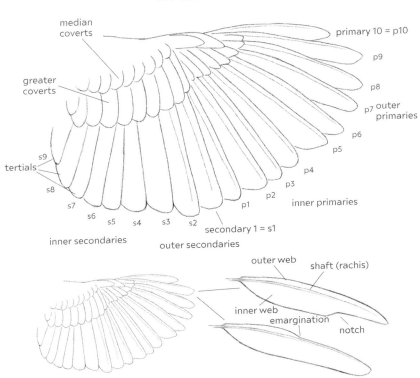

median coverts
primary 10 = p10
p9
p8
p7 outer primaries
greater coverts
p6
p5
p4
p3
p2
p1
inner primaries
s9
tertials
s8
s7
s6
s5
s4
s3
s2
secondary 1 = s1
inner secondaries
outer secondaries

outer web
shaft (rachis)
inner web
emargination
notch

13

Size, Shape, and Structure

Most *Myiarchus* and *Tyrannus* are similar in overall build, except for Fork-tailed and Scissor-tailed Flycatchers, which are usually unmistakable because of their long tails. Always note differences in bill size, and overall size and shape. Is it slim or barrel-chested? Does it have a big or small head? Is the head slightly crested or is it round? For example, among the *Myiarchus* flycatchers, Brown-crested is a large and stocky bird with a big bill, whereas Ash-throated is slightly smaller and slimmer, with a medium-sized bill. In kingbirds, Thick-billed has a hulking bill compared with Western and Cassin's. When perched, kingbirds often have a more horizontal posture and *Myiarchus* a more vertical posture.

   Primary projection, which is measured by how far the primaries extend beyond the longest tertial on a folded wing, can sometimes be useful. Western and Cassin's Kingbirds have much longer primary projections than other yellow-bellied kingbirds. *Myiarchus* all have relatively short primary projections compared with kingbirds.

   Differences in tail length, structure, and pattern within each genus are subtle. In kingbirds, the ***shape of the tail tip*** can be useful. Note whether the tip of the tail is squared off or slightly forked.

BODY SIZE AND SHAPE

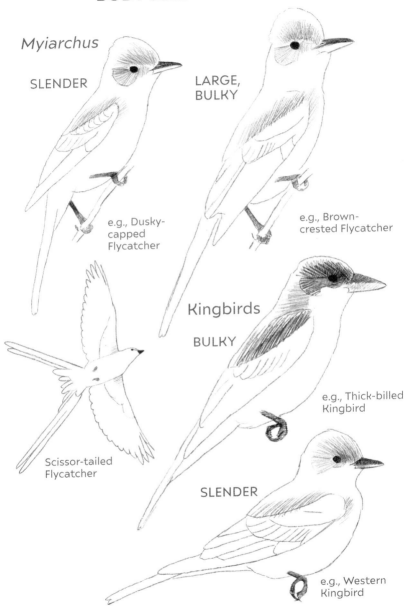

Myiarchus

SLENDER

e.g., Dusky-capped Flycatcher

LARGE, BULKY

e.g., Brown-crested Flycatcher

Scissor-tailed Flycatcher

Kingbirds

BULKY

e.g., Thick-billed Kingbird

SLENDER

e.g., Western Kingbird

15

PRIMARY PROJECTION

extreme birds are illustrated as there is some overlap

Tropical Kingbird

Western Kingbird

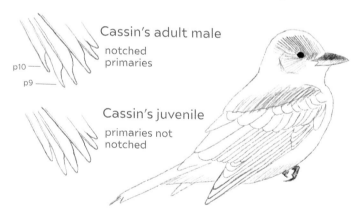

Cassin's adult male

notched
primaries

p10

p9

Cassin's juvenile

primaries not
notched

be careful when assessing as primary projection
appears longer with drooped wings

TAIL SHAPES

SQUARE/SLIGHTLY NOTCHED

e.g., Western Kingbird

DEEPLY FORKED

e.g., Tropical Kingbird

Overall Colors, Color Patterns, and Contrasts

All species of North American *Myiarchus* have very similar coloration, and our species of *Tyrannus* are also similar. It is thus important to focus on relative color contrasts. For example, in the yellow-bellied kingbirds, one should focus on the color of the chest compared with the belly. Cassin's and Western have grayer chests, but Cassin's chest contrasts more strongly with its yellow belly. Tropical and Couch's have yellower chests. In the white-bellied kingbirds, one should focus on contrast between the mantle and underparts, with Eastern Kingbird showing strong contrast and Gray showing weaker contrast. In *Myiarchus* flycatchers, pay attention to belly color, which can range from pale yellow in Ash-throated to bright yellow in Great Crested. All *Myiarchus* flycatchers have gray chests, but note the shade of gray, the degree of contrast between the gray chest and belly, and how far down the chest the gray extends. In *Myiarchus*, note whether there are subtle color contrasts between the crown, face, throat, and chest.

OVERALL COLORATION

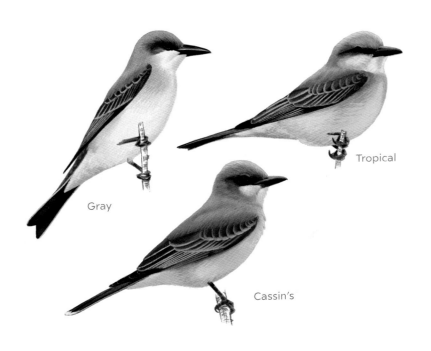

Gray

Tropical

Cassin's

La Sagra's

Ash-throated

Brown-crested

Great-crested

Wing Patterns

Make note of the color and brightness of the edges of wing feathers. Pay close attention to the median (upper wingbar) and greater covert (lower wingbar) edges, which define the boldness of the **wingbars**. Do the **wingbars contrast** with the wing ground color and the bird's back? Take note also of the *secondaries* and *primaries*. These flight feathers are typically pale edged, but in *Myiarchus*, note differences in color of pale edges. For example, in Ash-throated Flycatcher, primaries have rufous edges whereas secondaries have whitish edges, giving a strong *wing panel contrast*. In Dusky-capped Flycatcher, both secondary and primary feather edges are dull rufous or yellow, resulting in weak wing panel contrast. There may also be subtle differences in the color of secondary feather edges between inner and outer secondaries. For example, in Nutting's Flycatcher, secondary feather edges gradually grade upward (from outer to inner secondaries) from rufous to yellowish on the folded wing. In Brown-crested, the secondaries tend to be whitish except for the outermost (s1) secondary, which is often rufous. Subtle differences in wing panel contrast are also displayed between Tropical and Couch's Kingbirds. Finally, make note of the pale edges to the *tertials* (the innermost secondaries or top of the secondary stack on the folded wing). Great Crested Flycatcher, for example, has a bright and contrasting pale edge on the top tertial (innermost secondary).

WING PATTERNS

wingbar contrast with mantle and rest of wing

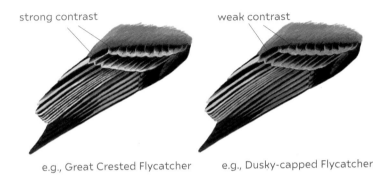

strong contrast

weak contrast

e.g., Great Crested Flycatcher

e.g., Dusky-capped Flycatcher

wing panel contrast between primaries and secondaries

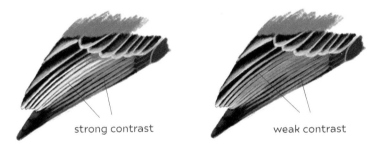

strong contrast

weak contrast

e.g., Ash-throated Flycatcher

e.g., Dusky-capped Flycatcher

Tail Patterns

In *Myiarchus* and kingbirds, it is important to pay attention to the color patterns of the tail. In kingbirds, note whether there are white outer margins to the tail or whether the tail feathers have white tips—these can be seen from both above and below. In *Myiarchus*, tail patterns are best seen from the underside. *Myiarchus* undertails range from extensively rufous to mostly dark. In those with rufous in the tail, the outer margins of the tail are dark, and the exact geometry of the dark outer margins on a folded undertail is often diagnostic of species.

These undertail patterns are defined by the color patterns of individual outer-tail feathers. In Western Kingbird, the outer web of the outermost tail feather (r6) is white, resulting in a narrow white margin or border to Western's black tail. *Myiarchus* tail feathers are variably patterned with rufous ***inner webs*** and dark ***outer webs***, but the extent to which the dark color of the outer web bleeds over to the inner web can be diagnostic. For example, in Ash-throated Flycatcher, the dark outer web hooks inward at the tip of the feather, resulting in a dark-tipped tail. In Great Crested and Brown-crested Flycatchers, the dark outer web rarely crosses the shaft into the inner web, and most birds have a straight and narrow dark outer margin to the folded tail, all the way to the tip. In Dusky-capped Flycatcher, the underside of the tail usually appears completely dark, because the outer web and much of the inner web of its tail feathers are dark.

When assessing tail patterns, it is important to note age and time of year. In worn kingbirds (often in late summer), white outer margins to the tail can be worn away or feather edges frayed giving the appearance of white outer margins, especially on backlit birds. Juvenile *Myiarchus* flycatchers often have more extensive rufous in their tails.

TAIL PATTERN

underside

Kingbirds

Tropical   Western   Cassin's   Eastern

Myiarchus

Brown-crested   Ash-throated   Dusky-capped

Vocalizations

The vocalizations of kingbirds and *Myiarchus* flycatchers are often distinct enough to be separated in the field with a little practice. In each species account, we display spectrograms and mnemonics to help one visualize, learn, and remember how a bird sounds. To complement these spectrograms, the reader should refer to online sound repositories such as the Macaulay Library of Sounds at the Cornell Laboratory of Ornithology and xeno-canto.org.

In a spectrogram, the horizontal axis represents time, and the vertical axis represents frequency. The boldness of the spectrogram represents the sound's amplitude (loudness). When listening to vocalizations and studying spectrograms, always note whether a call note is rising or descending in frequency or monotonic (flat), which part of a call note is louder or more accented, the number of syllables in a call, and how long a call note is. The length of a mnemonic is an attempt to represent the length of a call note. Capital letters are used to emphasize which part of a call or song is accented.

To illustrate, "*pip*" and "*whit*" call notes are typically shorter than one second. A "*whit*" is represented by a rising spectrogram, with a soft "*whit*" showing a slight inflection and a sharp "*whit*" being steep. A "*pip*" is represented by a narrow and peaked (or upside down "V") spectrogram. Slurs or whistled calls are represented by thin (narrow frequency range) and long spectrograms. Burry call notes are represented by fuzzy or modulated (broad frequency band) spectrograms. A "*peeeuu*" describes the more drawn-out slurred call note of Dusky-capped. A "*weEEP*" describes the rising call note of Great Crested. A "*brEEEerrr*" describes the rising and then descending burry call of a Couch's Kingbird. Any given species can give a variety of call notes. Call notes can be given in isolation, or repeated slowly or in very rapid succession (e.g., twitter) over several seconds (>3 notes per second).

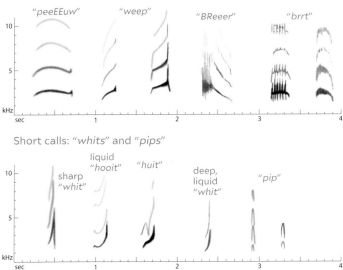

Long drawn-out calls

"peeEEuw"   "weep"   "BReeer"   "brrt"

Short calls: "whits" and "pips"

liquid
"hooit"   "huit"
sharp
"whit"   deep,
liquid   "pip"
"whit"

Kingbird and *Myiarchus* flycatcher songs are not melodic in the classic sense but nonetheless can be musical. Songs are short to long series of notes made by repeating and combining different call notes. Remembering songs may seem challenging, but because songs incorporate many call notes, familiarity with call notes can help you recognize them in a song. In deciphering songs, it is also important to note the overall quality of the song. Is the song monotonic or does it undulate in frequency, giving it a rolling rhythmic quality? Does the song include burry notes ("*brrr*"), rising "*weeps*," short "*pip*" notes, or twittering phrases? Does the song's tempo accelerate or increase in amplitude toward the end?

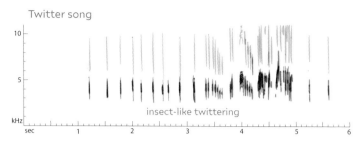

Twitter song

insect-like twittering

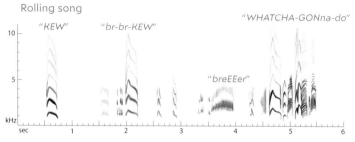

Rolling song

"KEW" "br-br-KEW" "WHATCHA-GONna-do"

"breEEer"

For any bird of uncertain identification, efforts should be made to record vocalizations. Fancy equipment is not needed as almost any smartphone's recorder and microphone are sufficient. Playing back recordings of a flycatcher may sometimes entice a bird to respond, but beware that flycatchers and kingbirds sometimes respond to vocalizations of other species, and sometimes not at all. Playback should be used sparingly to avoid disturbing a bird for any longer than to gauge a response. Given the ease and popularity of using bird sound apps for playback and recording in the field, there is a real risk that birds are overstimulated in popular birding areas. There is also the risk of confusion if audio playback from another observer is accidentally recorded onto the same file as a bird's actual vocalizations.

Age and Molt

Myiarchus flycatchers and kingbirds are virtually identical in appearance between sexes and at different times of the year. However, there are subtle differences in plumage that result from molt, and the wear and tear on feathers. Flycatchers replace worn feathers on an annual cycle.

Juvenal plumage refers to the plumage of immature birds when they leave the nest, beginning their first annual cycle of life. In most flycatchers, this plumage is nearly identical to the **adult plumage**, but the edges of the tail, wing coverts, primaries, and secondaries may be more brightly colored yellow or buff. For example, juvenal secondary feather edges and tertials in *Myiarchus* flycatchers are brighter yellow or rufous. Juvenal plumage kingbirds and *Myiarchus* may also have slightly brighter wingbars than adults. The tails of juvenal plumaged *Myiarchus* typically have more extensive rufous than those of adults.

In its first fall and winter, the immature or first-cycle bird will undergo an incomplete molt, termed the **preformative molt** (this term applies only to first-cycle birds and is often referred to as the first prebasic molt in other texts), after which it attains its formative plumage (referred to as the first basic plumage in other texts). The preformative molt involves mostly body feathers and a limited number of flight and tail feathers. Many juvenal flight and tail feathers are retained through the preformative molt so that in spring these first-cycle birds will show a mixture of old (juvenal) and new (formative) flight feathers in the wing. The new formative feathers will appear fresh, while the retained juvenal feathers will appear more worn.

At the beginning of a bird's second year of life, it will undergo another post-nesting season molt, typically in the fall and winter for Northern Hemisphere birds. This molt (and all subsequent fall/winter molts) is termed the **prebasic molt**, after which the bird acquires its adult plumage (**basic plumage**). Unlike the preformative molt in first-cycle birds, the prebasic molt in adults is usually

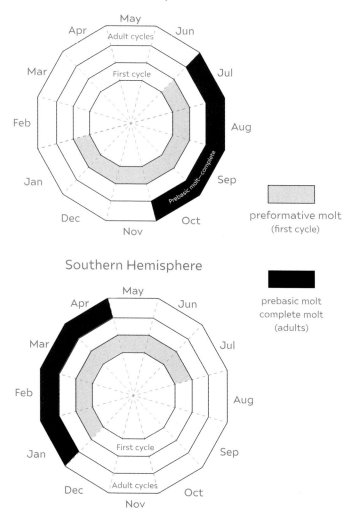

Northern Hemisphere

Adult cycles
First cycle
Prebasic molt—complete

May · Jun · Jul · Aug · Sep · Oct · Nov · Dec · Jan · Feb · Mar · Apr

preformative molt
(first cycle)

Southern Hemisphere

First cycle
Adult cycles

May · Jun · Jul · Aug · Sep · Oct · Nov · Dec · Jan · Feb · Mar · Apr

prebasic molt
complete molt
(adults)

Generalized molt cycles. Inner cycle represents first-cycle birds. Outer cycle represents adults; that is, any bird from its second full year of life onward. Immature birds (first cycle) go through an incomplete preformative molt in the late summer and fall (gray). Adults go through a complete prebasic molt, beginning in late summer and completing in the fall on wintering grounds (solid black). Most of this book focuses on a Northern Hemisphere perspective of molt, with birds born between May and June. Southern Hemisphere birds molt late in the austral summer. For simplicity, prealternate molt is not shown.

complete, with all flight feathers replaced. In most flycatchers and kingbirds, the prebasic molt tends to be protracted, beginning with molt of body plumage on breeding grounds, but mostly completing on wintering grounds with replacement of flight feathers (with some molt occurring on migratory stopovers). Exceptions are Scissor-tailed and Great Crested Flycatcher, which typically complete most of their prebasic molt on summering grounds before heading south.

Flycatchers of all ages may go through a limited molt just before the breeding season. This is known as the **prealternate molt**, but the molt is limited mostly to body feathers, rarely including flight or tail feathers.

The extent of feather wear can be useful in aging and identification. In the fall, first-cycle birds will typically appear fresh (crisp and unfrayed feather edges), especially in the wing, because the flight and covert feathers were generated only a few months ago. Adults just prior to the prebasic molt (late summer and early fall) will have worn or frayed flight and tail feathers as these feathers bear witness to a year of wear and tear. Because the replacement of flight feathers is usually completed on wintering grounds, adults will appear worn, particularly in the wing, in late summer or during fall migration in the United States. Thus, fresh birds in Aug. and Sept. are likely immature birds, whereas during this time worn birds are likely adults. Because they complete their prebasic molts on summering grounds, adult Great Crested and Scissor-tailed Flycatchers appear fresh during southbound migration.

In the spring, difference in wear and tear on feathers reverses. Because birds in their first year retain some juvenal flight feathers through the preformative and prealternate molts, their plumage may show a mixture of new and worn juvenal feathers. In particular, in spring, the wings of first-cycle birds may show worn juvenal feathers and some fresh and unworn outer primaries (resulting in different generations of feathers being present in the wing simultaneously). By contrast, adults will have replaced all their flight feathers in the fall/winter, so in spring their feathers are younger than first-cycle feathers and thus will appear fresher than the feathers of first-cycle birds.

The foregoing discussions on calendar timing of molts pertain to birds that breed in the Northern Hemisphere and winter in the tropics. For migratory birds that breed in the Southern Hemisphere (austral migrants), such as some subspecies of the Tropical Kingbird and Fork-tailed Flycatcher, the discussions still apply except that calendar years for a season are flipped. That is, austral migrants breed during the northern winters. Post-breeding dispersal and migration of austral migrants happen in the austral fall, which corresponds to the northern spring. Vagrants in North America in the northern spring may be immatures embarking on their first austral fall migration.

Paying close attention to the freshness of feathers is important for making a correct identification because the same species may look different when fresh or worn. Under worn conditions (usually just before the prebasic molt in adults), the bright pale edges to the primaries, secondaries, wing coverts (wingbars), and tail can often be frayed or all but worn away. Frayed feathers may give the appearance of pale fringes to feathers. Cassin's Kingbirds with worn tail feathers might show extensively pale outer-tail margins, especially when backlit, whereas a worn Western Kingbird might have reduced or even absent white outer-tail margins.

Behavior

Like many members of the flycatcher family, *Myiarchus* and kingbirds catch their insect prey on the wing by sallying out from a perch, often returning to the same perch. However, they differ from the smaller and more nervous *Empidonax* flycatchers in that they rarely flick their wings or tails. At best, they may occasionally pump their tails. *Myiarchus* and kingbirds are a photographer's ideal birds because of their calm and approachable nature.

When observing the behavior of *Myiarchus* and kingbirds, focus on where they forage or perch. For example, kingbirds typically sit on prominently exposed perches, such as tall dead snags, powerlines, fences, and signposts. Some *Myiarchus*, like Ash-throated and Brown-crested flycatchers, also sit on somewhat exposed branches and structures, but may retreat into the interior of shrubs and trees when not feeding. Other *Myiarchus*, like Dusky-capped and Nutting's, are on the shier side. They tend to perch on branches beneath the canopy or protruding from the edges of shrubs. Great Crested prefers to feed under the canopy of tall deciduous trees. Interestingly, Myiarchus flycatchers often crane their necks out, giving the appearance of peering.

Breeding season behavior may also be worth noting. Kingbirds showing territorial behavior often fly high in the air and hover, making twittering or chattering calls. Kingbirds are also known for aggressively chasing or harassing potential threats, such as raptors and corvids. Male kingbirds often participate in aggressive aerial fights with each other. *Myiarchus* flycatchers do not perform such conspicuous aerial displays but can still be rather aggressive to potential threats.

Both *Myiarchus* and kingbirds are highly vocal during the breeding season, especially at dawn. In some, like kingbirds, singing may even begin a couple of hours before dawn. Listening to the pre-dawn chorus of kingbirds calling is always an unforgettable experience.

There are also interesting differences in flocking or social behavior. *Myiarchus* flycathers are solitary except when paired up in the breeding season. Kingbirds appear to be more social. Cassin's Kingbirds may nest in relative proximity to each other. In the nonbreeding season, some kingbird species congregate. Cassin's Kingbirds often associate in loose groups in winter. Eastern Kingbirds move in flocks of ten to hundreds along the Texas coast during migration. In the upper Amazon, wintering flocks of Eastern Kingbirds can number in the thousands. Western Kingbirds and Scissor-tailed Flycatchers migrate in small groups of ten to 20, often congregating together along the coast. Migrating groups of kingbirds may attract other species of kingbirds. Vagrant Fork-tailed Flycatchers have been found with flocks of Scissor-tailed Flycatchers. Vagrant Tropical Kingbirds may show up with migrating Western or Cassin's Kingbirds.

Habitat

There are subtle differences between species in habitat and climate preferences. Unlike *Empidonax* flycatchers, many *Myiarchus* and kingbirds are found strictly in subtropical to tropical climates. Probably because these birds prey on larger insects (grasshoppers, cicadas, and butterflies) and small reptiles, they tend to avoid cold climates and habitats, where such prey are scarce. Even for those whose breeding range extends to higher latitudes, such as the Ash-throated Flycatcher, and Western and Eastern Kingbirds in the United States, their distribution is restricted to low elevations or foothills, where it is warmer. The higher elevation coniferous forests are generally avoided. In the eastern United States, the northern limit of the Great Crested Flycatcher's range is demarcated by the transition from the warmer and more humid eastern deciduous forests to the coniferous forests of southern Canada.

When observing a flycatcher, one should make note of the overall density and structure of a habitat's vegetation. Is the bird found in open habitats (e.g., savannas, agricultural fields, etc.), semi-open habitats (e.g., thorn scrub, open woodlands, chaparral, and woodland edges), or forested areas? Is the habitat near water, such as a lake, or along a riparian corridor or slow-moving river?

Most kingbirds (*Tyrannus*) favor open to semi-open habitats, such as savannas, farmlands, fields, deserts, and woodland edges, where they often sit conspicuously on exposed structures like fence posts, powerlines, tall dead snags, or at the tops of trees or shrubs. Yet there are subtle differences in habitat preference among the kingbirds. For example, in very open habitats, one is likely only to encounter Western Kingbirds, and Scissor-tailed and Fork-tailed Flycatchers. Mature riparian areas surrounded by grasslands, chaparral, or thorn scrub are also frequented by Western Kingbirds and, especially, by Thick-billed Kingbirds. Cassin's Kingbirds tend to avoid very open habitats, preferring semi-open vegetation, such as oak savannas, mixed oak-pine foothill woodlands, riparian edges, and suburban parklands. Some kingbirds, such as Couch's and Tropical, can be found in open and semi-open habitats, but often like to be near water bodies, such as lakes or slow-moving rivers. Gray and Loggerhead Kingbirds prefer tropical woodlands along the coast. Kingbirds are often attracted to bees and beehives, and in the winter, may frequent trees with small berries.

Myiarchus flycatchers inhabit a variety of habitats. Ash-throated frequents open habitats as long as there are scattered bushes or tall cacti. Ash-throated also frequents open woodlands of the western United States, including chaparral, thorn scrub, mixed pine-oak woodlands, and riparian corridors. Brown-crested is found in similar habitats to Ash-throated, but generally requires larger trees as a key component of their habitat. In our region, Brown-crested is strictly confined to the deserts of southwestern United States and southern Texas. Nutting's Flycatcher also prefers semi-open areas, but a scattering of dense vegetation is required as this shy bird tends to feed more from within low vegetation than other *Myiarchus* species. At the other extreme is the Great Crested Flycatcher, which requires forests with tall trees, especially deciduous trees. Great Crested tends to avoid open habitats, except around woodland edges. Dusky-capped also prefers woodlands or woodland edges, from pine-oak and riparian woodlands to thorn scrub.

It is worth noting that *Myiarchus* flycatchers are secondary cavity nesters, which means that they generally require woodpecker holes to nest in. Thus, although some *Myiarchus* can be found in semi-open habitats, some large trees or giant cacti are necessary for nesting. Some *Myiarchus*, like Ash-throated, may take advantage of human-made cavities, such as holes in pipes or fence posts, for example. Kingbird nests are loose structures placed in the crotches of trees or, in some cases, human-made structures like utility poles.

Oak-sycamore woodlands in lower Madera canyon, located in the foothills of the Santa Rita Mountains in southeastern Arizona. These dry woodland canyons provide ideal habitats for Cassin's Kingbirds and Dusky-capped Flycatchers. Brown-crested and Ash-throated flycatchers also frequent these habitats.

Oak woodlands in the foothills of the Santa Rita Mountains in southeastern Arizona. Brown-crested, Ash-throated, and Dusky-capped Flycatchers, and Cassin's Kingbirds, can be found in this habitat.

Desert thorn scrub (mesquite) and giant cactus (Saguaro) woodlands in the Sonoran Desert near Tucson, Arizona. These habitats are frequented by Ash-throated and Brown-crested Flycatchers, and Western Kingbirds. Woodpecker holes in giant cacti are often used as nesting sites for *Myiarchus* flycatchers.

Riparian habitats in the Mojave Desert in southern California. Cottonwood and willow riparian woodlands are frequented by Ash-throated and Brown-crested Flycatchers as well as Western Kingbirds.

Riparian woodlands with cottonwoods and willows along the slow-moving Santa Cruz River in southeastern Arizona. Thick-billed and Western Kingbirds, and Ash-throated and Brown-crested Flycatchers nest in these habitats.

Open oak woodlands near Arivaca in southeastern Arizona are favored by Cassin's Kingbirds and Ash-throated Flycatchers.

In coastal California, suburban woodlands and parks with live oaks, sycamores, and non-native trees, such as eucalyptus, are often where Cassin's Kingbirds can be found. Ash-throated Flycatcher and Western Kingbird also nest in these habitats. Vagrant Thick-billed Kingbirds in coastal California are typically found in suburban park settings.

Riparian woodlands along slow-moving rivers and lakes in South Texas provide habitat for Tropical and Couch's Kingbirds.

Brushy grasslands and thorn scrub edges in south Texas are frequented by Couch's and Western Kingbirds as well as Scissor-tailed Flycatchers. Kingbirds often perch on powerlines.

Grasslands and agricultural areas with scattered trees are the favored haunts of Scissor-tailed Flycatchers (in Texas and Oklahoma) and Eastern Kingbirds (in eastern North America).

Deciduous hardwood forests of eastern North America provide habitat for Great Crested Flycatchers. Point Pelee, Ontario.

Deciduous forests of the southeastern United States are frequented by Great Crested Flycatchers. East Texas.

Range, Seasonal Status and Migration

Unlike *Empidonax* and some *Contopus* pewees, whose breeding ranges extend into the boreal forests of Canada and Alaska, the breeding ranges of kingbirds and *Myiarchus* are more southerly: no further north than southern Canada. Many have breeding ranges primarily within the subtropics, and subtropical and tropical latitudes have the highest diversity of kingbirds and *Myiarchus*. Species diversity is greater in the western part of the United States compared with the east, where only the Great Crested Flycatcher and Eastern Kingbird are regular breeders.

Kingbirds and *Myiarchus* flycatchers are not a homogeneous group when it comes to migratory patterns. Most kingbirds and *Myiarchus* are short-distance migrants, migrating from breeding grounds in the United States to their wintering grounds in Mexico and Central America. Some of the lower latitude species, like Nutting's and Dusky-capped Flycatcher and several kingbirds (Thick-billed, Couch's, and Tropical) are largely resident in Mexico and Central America and only show local range expansions for breeding. Caribbean flycatchers and kingbirds are largely resident or only show local movements. Our only long-distance migrants are the Eastern Kingbird and Great Crested Flycatcher, which winter in the eastern Andes and upper Amazon of South America, respectively.

Range maps with charts showing migration timing accompany each species account. Purple corresponds to year-round status, orange to the breeding range, blue to the nonbreeding range and yellow to the migratory range. We have color-coded maps in terms of breeding, nonbreeding, and migratory ranges rather than by calendar season (e.g., fall, winter, spring, summer) because some birds range into the Southern Hemisphere where seasons are reversed relative to the Northern Hemisphere. In the Northern Hemisphere, breeding usually takes place from Apr. to July, whereas wintering occurs primarily from Oct. to Mar. For Southern Hemisphere birds, such as the South American subspecies of Brown-crested and Fork-tailed

Flycatchers and Tropical Kingbird, breeding and wintering take place in the corresponding periods of the austral year.

We have provided seasonal abundance charts in the form of bar graphs to illustrate migration (green) timing at representative locations or the probability of encountering a vagrant bird (red). In the range map, contour lines show arrival times for fall and spring migrants. Contours are shown with two-week intervals (biweekly): the beginning of the month is defined by a solid contour and the exact middle of the month by a dashed contour. Careful attention should be paid to arrival times as flycatchers and kingbirds tend to be faithful to arrival and departure dates from year to year. Fall birds may occasionally linger beyond the dates noted on the map or bar charts.

In some cases, we have drawn arrows depicting approximate migration routes. Flycatchers and kingbirds of western North America typically follow the north–south trending mountain ranges characteristic of western North America. In most cases, arrival on northwestern breeding grounds, such as along the Pacific coast, is earlier than the same species' arrival in the mountains of the continental interior (Montana, Colorado, Utah) because the rise in temperatures in these interior mountains in spring lag behind those of the more humid Pacific coast. Eastern flycatchers and kingbirds mostly migrate around the Gulf of Mexico, such as along the western coast of the Gulf of Mexico via southern Texas or by hopping across the Caribbean islands between Florida and Central America. Trans-Gulf of Mexico migration between Louisiana and the Yucatan Peninsula probably also occurs, but more work is needed to sort out the details.

Not surprisingly, vagrancy is frequently associated with first-cycle birds, which are less experienced. Thus, it is no surprise that the highest probability of finding a vagrant in North America is during the northern fall when young birds are embarking on their first migration. Most of the vagrant Tropical Kingbirds to the Pacific and Atlantic coasts are immatures, as are vagrant Great Crested Flycatchers to the Pacific coast. Southern Hemisphere birds are also prone to vagrancy. Post-breeding dispersal of Southern Hemisphere birds happens between Mar. and May, when they move north to their equatorial nonbreeding range. Some of these birds may overshoot and find themselves in North America. These are technically fall vagrants from a Southern Hemisphere perspective, but they turn up in the spring of North America.

GENERIC FLYCATCHER

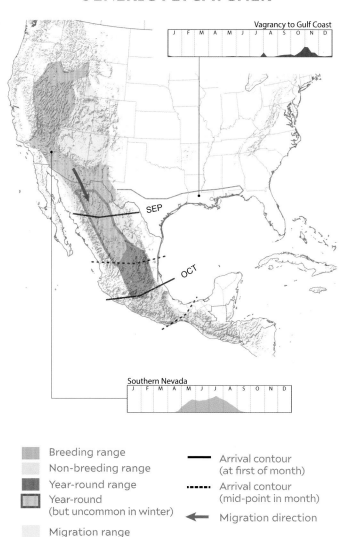

Vagrancy to Gulf Coast
J F M A M J J A S O N D

SEP

OCT

Southern Nevada
J F M A M J J A S O N D

Breeding range
Non-breeding range
Year-round range
Year-round
(but uncommon in winter)
Migration range
Vagrancy range

—— Arrival contour
(at first of month)
▪▪▪▪▪▪ Arrival contour
(mid-point in month)
← Migration direction

Myiarchus
Flycatchers

Myiarchus Flycatchers
Identifying Myiarchus *flycatchers*

The *Myiarchus* flycatchers are medium to large members of the tyrant flycatcher family. They have duller coloring than kingbirds, but are more brightly colored than *Empidonax* flycatchers. *Myiarchus* flycatchers are generally gray to brown with yellowish underparts. The primary and often the secondary feathers in *Myiarchus* have bright outer edges, ranging from rufous to yellow. The tail feathers of most *Myiarchus* show some rufous on the inner web. Unlike *Empidonax*, *Myiarchus* flycatchers do not flick their wings or tails. *Myiarchus* flycatchers tend to perch less conspicuously than kingbirds, preferring perches beneath forest canopy or within and on the exterior of small trees and shrubs. Unlike kingbirds, the *Myiarchus* flycatchers do not form social groups. The next sections highlight the points to focus on when encountering a *Myiarchus*.

Size, Shape, and Structure

Body size and shape. *Myiarchus* species are generally similar in shape and structure, but note overall size and shape of a bird. For example, Brown-crested is large, big headed, and has a bulky body. Dusky-capped and La Sagra's have smaller, slimmer bodies. From largest to smallest, the *Myiarchus* flycatchers follow this sequence: Brown-crested, Great Crested, Ash-throated, Nutting's, Dusky-capped, La Sagra's Flycatcher. Beware of overlap between species.

   Tail length. All *Myiarchus* have long tails, but there are subtle differences in tail length and shape. Great Crested has the shortest and widest tail. Dusky-capped has a proportionately longer and narrower tail. Narrow tails often narrow toward the body, whereas wider tails, like Great Crested, do not narrow as much toward the body. Of course, these features depend on how the bird is holding its tail, and there is overlap between species.

MYIARCHUS COMPARISON

La Sagra's

Dusky-capped

Nutting's

Ash-throated

Great Crested

Brown-crested

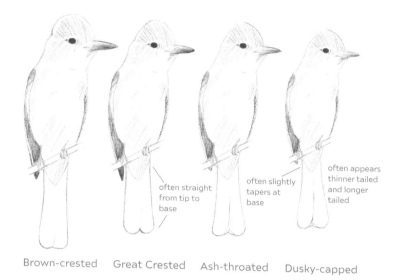

often straight from tip to base

often slightly tapers at base

often appears thinner tailed and longer tailed

Brown-crested   Great Crested   Ash-throated   Dusky-capped

Bill size and shape. Make note of relative bill size as there are subtle differences. Brown-crested has the largest and thickest bill. Dusky-capped and La Sagra's have the thinnest bills. Note the shape of the bill, especially that of the culmen on the upper mandible. Dusky-capped's bill is thin with a straighter culmen, whereas Brown-crested's bill has a thicker base and slightly more curved culmen. Ash-throated is intermediate in terms of bill characteristics. As in many field marks related to flycatchers, it is important to note that differences in bill size are subtle, and there is slight overlap between certain species. Finally, note whether the base of the bill (where the bill meets the head) is pale or dark. Great Crested and Brown-crested can often show slightly pale bases to the bill.

note that bill length can be variable e.g., Great Crested, Ash-throated and Brown-crested *cooperi* can overlap

Brown-crested *magister*

Ash-throated

Great Crested

Nutting's

Brown-crested *cooperi*

Dusky-capped

La Sagra's

Crown shape. All *Myiarchus* have a slightly crested or peaked crown, but Dusky-capped and Nutting's tend to show slightly rounder crowns compared with Great Crested, Ash-throated, and Brown-crested. Note, however, that crown shape overlaps between species and may vary depending on a bird's posture.

CROWN SHAPES

Round

e.g., Dusky-capped Flycatcher

Peaked

e.g., Brown-crested Flycatcher

Dusky-capped with crown raised

Primary projection. *Myiarchus* flycatchers have relatively short primary projections compared with other tyrant flycatchers. However, subtle differences exist. Great Crested typically has the longest primary projection of *Myiarchus*, presumably because it is a long-distance migrant. La Sagra's, a relatively nonmigratory bird, has the shortest primary projection. Ash-throated's primary projection is intermediate. Primary projection should never be used alone for identification as there is overlap between species, but it can sometimes be a useful supporting field mark at the extremes.

PRIMARY PROJECTION

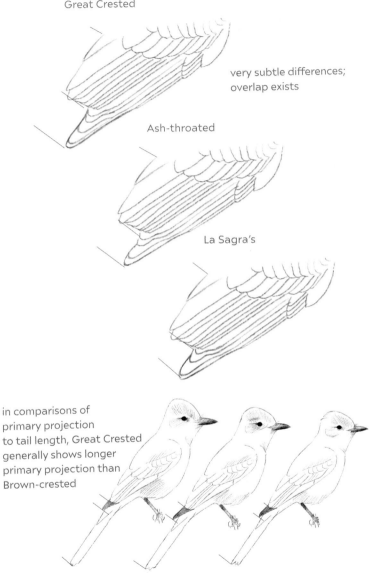

Great Crested

very subtle differences;
overlap exists

Ash-throated

La Sagra's

in comparisons of
primary projection
to tail length, Great Crested
generally shows longer
primary projection than
Brown-crested

Brown-crested   Great Crested   Ash-throated

Body Coloration and Plumage Contrasts

Intensity of yellow underparts. Although *Myiarchus* species are overall similar in body coloration, note how yellow the underparts are, and how dark the upperparts are. Great Crested has bright yellow underparts, Ash-throated has pale yellow underparts, and La Sagra's has whitish underparts. Dusky-capped and Great Crested have dark gray or brown upperparts, whereas Ash-throated has light gray-brown upperparts.

Chest contrast. In all *Myiarchus*, yellow underparts are confined to the belly, but the chest shows different shades of gray, generating different levels of contrast between the chest and belly. Make note of how dark the chest is, how far the gray extends down from the chest, and how much the chest contrasts with the yellow belly. Great Crested has a dark gray chest, but other species of *Myiarchus* have lighter gray chests. The gray on Great Crested is confined to the upper chest, but in Ash-throated, the gray extends to the lower chest before gradually transitioning into yellow. Make note of how sharp the transition between the gray chest and yellow belly is; for example, it is gradual and diffuse in Ash-throated and more demarcated in Great Crested.

Head and face color patterns. Note the darkness of the crown, face, and throat relative to each other and to the gray chest. Are they concolorous or are they of slightly different color or darkness? Dusky-capped's crown and face are both dark, but the throat is pale and the chest intermediate, resulting in strong contrast between crown/face and throat/chest. In Ash-throated and Brown-crested, the face is intermediate gray, the crown is darker, and the throat lighter. Great Crested's crown, face, throat, and chest have similar gray coloring, resulting in less contrast and giving it a strong hooded appearance.

Body Coloration

La Sagra's   Ash-throated   Brown-crested   Nutting's   Dusky-capped   Great Crested

Chest Contrast

STRONG CHEST CONTRAST
Great Crested

INTERMEDIATE
Dusky-capped

WEAK
Ash-throated

Face Contrast

crown

face

throat

Dusky-capped   Ash-throated   Great Crested

Undertail Pattern and Color

Myiarchus flycatchers have variable amounts of rufous in their tails, ranging from limited to almost no rufous in La Sagra's and Dusky-capped to extensive rufous in Great Crested, Ash-throated, Nutting's, and Brown-crested. In those with extensive rufous, the outer-tail feathers have a dark brown **outer margin** (mostly on the **outer web** of the feather shaft) that often contrasts with a rufous **inner web** (on the inside of the shaft). The exact pattern of individual outer-tail feathers can be difficult to discern in the field unless the bird fans its tail long enough to be photographed. From above, all folded tails look dark because the inner webs of the outer-tail feathers are hidden beneath the central tail feathers. Make every attempt to observe the undertail because these outer-tail patterns are most easily seen from below.

The undertails of Brown-crested and Great Crested are characterized by a straight dark brown outer margin, with the rufous center of the undertail continuing all the way to the tip of the tail. Great Crested's dark outer margin is narrow and confined to the outer web (outside of feather shaft) whereas Brown-crested has a slightly broader outer margin (bleeding slightly over the shaft and into the inner web).

In Ash-throated and Nutting's, the dark outer-tail margins hook or widen inward toward the tip of the tail, bleeding into the inner web. In Ash-throated, the hooking is complete, resulting in a terminal bar across the tip of the folded undertail. In Nutting's, the dark outer margin of the outer-tail feathers widens toward the tip but does not cross the tip of the tail.

In Dusky-capped and La Sagra's, the outer-tail feathers are mostly dark, with rufous confined to the edges of the inner web. In these species, the undertail will often appear completely dark in the field.

Finally, note that for all species, juvenile tail feathers may show more extensive rufous than adults. This is most pronounced for juvenile Ash-throated, in which the extent of terminal hooking is diminished.

MYIARCHUS UNDERTAILS

There can be variation; in general, juveniles have more rufous

ad   juv

The outer-tail feather (R6) is the most visible feather from below

Ash-throated

dark brown usually hooks around tip

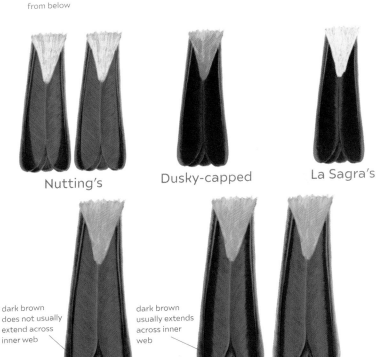

Nutting's

Dusky-capped

La Sagra's

dark brown does not usually extend across inner web

Great Crested

dark brown usually extends across inner web

Brown-crested

Wingbar Contrast

Wingbars are generally not conspicuous in *Myiarchus* flycatchers, but subtle differences exist. The extent of paleness to the edges of the median (upper wingbar) and greater covert feathers (lower wingbar) determines how conspicuous the wingbars are. A good way to assess the strength of the contrast is to compare wingbar brightness to the ground color of the wing and mantle. At one extreme is the Dusky-capped Flycatcher, which has very dull or nonexistent wingbars, showing little contrast with the mantle. On the other extreme is Great Crested, which shows bright wingbars (for a *Myiarchus*) that stand out against the mantle and wing. Note that wear, tear, and age can influence the boldness of wingbars and tertial edgings, and that primary coverts can be light brown to rufous on first- and second-year birds.

WINGBAR CONTRAST

wingbar contrast with mantle and rest of wing

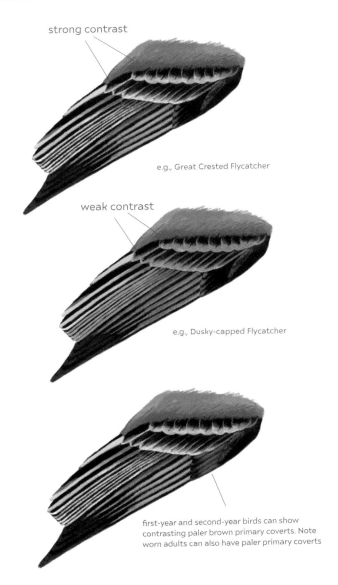

strong contrast

e.g., Great Crested Flycatcher

weak contrast

e.g., Dusky-capped Flycatcher

first-year and second-year birds can show
contrasting paler brown primary coverts. Note
worn adults can also have paler primary coverts

Wing Panel Contrast

Pay close attention also to the *secondary* and *primary panels*. These are the stacks of flight feathers on the folded wing. Both the secondaries and primaries have pale edges to their outer margins, but secondary and primary feather edges may differ in color, resulting in different contrast between secondary and primary wing panels (**wing panel contrast**). In Ash-throated Flycatcher, primaries have rufous edges whereas secondaries have whitish edges, giving a strong wing panel contrast (although juvenal Ash-throated may have rufous in secondaries). In Dusky-capped, both secondary and primary feather edges are dull rufous or yellow, resulting in weak wingbar contrast. In Nutting's, secondary feather edges grade upward from rufous to yellowish on the folded wing. Note that secondaries in juvenal plumage are often more rufous than in adult plumage. This is especially the case for Ash-throated and Great Crested.

WING PANEL CONTRAST

wing panel contrast between primaries and secondaries

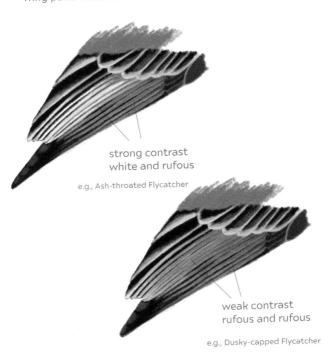

strong contrast
white and rufous

e.g., Ash-throated Flycatcher

weak contrast
rufous and rufous

e.g., Dusky-capped Flycatcher

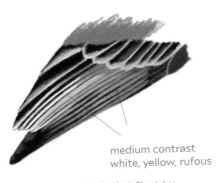

medium contrast
white, yellow, rufous

e.g., Nutting's Flycatcher

Vocalizations

The most reliable way to identify a *Myiarchus* is by voice. Songs are made up of a series of call notes, so learning the call notes is recommended. In nonbreeding season, calls may be the only vocalizations given.

Calls can be classified into long (>0.5 s) and short (<0.5 s) calls. Long calls are best described as long, drawn-out notes. They can be pewee-like, as in the mournful "*peeEEuew*" of Dusky-capped Flycatcher or the more cheerful and rising "*weep*" notes of Nutting's and Great Crested. Ash-throated, Brown-crested, and La Sagra's do not give long call notes.

Short calls come in liquid "*whit*" notes, burry notes, and emphatic "*pip*" notes. Dusky-capped and Nutting's do not give burry calls, but all other *Myiarchus* do. Some *Myiarchus* give "*pip*" calls (Ash-throated, Great Crested, and Brown-crested), but others do not (Dusky-capped, Nutting's, and La Sagra's). All *Myiarchus* give a variety of "*whit*" calls except for Ash-throated. There are subtle differences between the "*whit*" calls of different species. When listening to a "*whit*," take notice of whether it is sharp and emphatic or more liquid. Use the call chart to help you identify your bird.

MYIARCHUS CALL NOTES

Long calls: *"weep"* and *"peeEEuw"*

Short calls: *"whit"*

Short calls: *"pip"*

Short calls: *"brrt"*

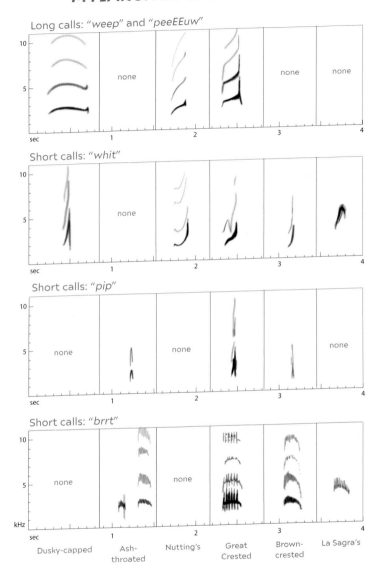

MYIARCHUS COMPARISON

(regularly occuring in US and Canada)

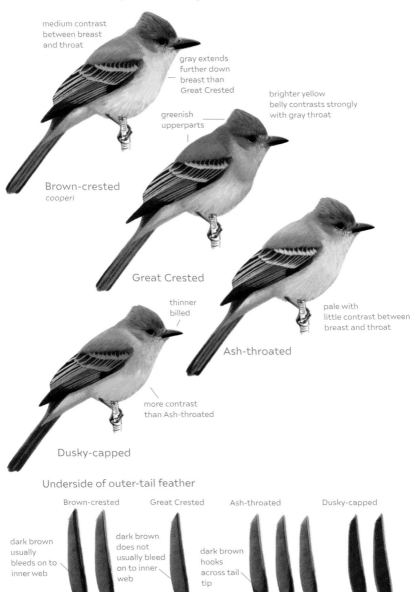

medium contrast
between breast
and throat

gray extends
further down
breast than
Great Crested

brighter yellow
belly contrasts strongly
with gray throat

greenish
upperparts

Brown-crested
cooperi

Great Crested

thinner
billed

pale with
little contrast between
breast and throat

Ash-throated

more contrast
than Ash-throated

Dusky-capped

Underside of outer-tail feather

Brown-crested   Great Crested   Ash-throated   Dusky-capped

dark brown
usually
bleeds on to
inner web

dark brown
does not
usually bleed
on to inner
web

dark brown
hooks
across tail
tip

ad   juv   ad   ad   ad   juv   ad   juv

MYIARCHUS COMPARISON

(regularly occuring in US and Canada)

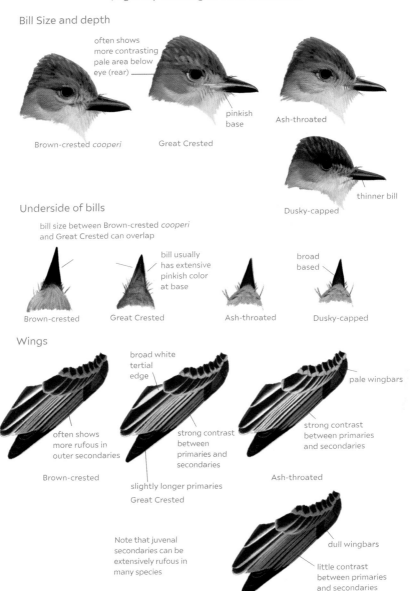

Bill Size and depth

often shows more contrasting pale area below eye (rear)

pinkish base

Ash-throated

Brown-crested *cooperi*

Great Crested

thinner bill

Dusky-capped

Underside of bills

bill size between Brown-crested *cooperi* and Great Crested can overlap

bill usually has extensive pinkish color at base

broad based

Brown-crested

Great Crested

Ash-throated

Dusky-capped

Wings

broad white tertial edge

pale wingbars

often shows more rufous in outer secondaries

strong contrast between primaries and secondaries

strong contrast between primaries and secondaries

Brown-crested

slightly longer primaries

Ash-throated

Great Crested

Note that juvenal secondaries can be extensively rufous in many species

dull wingbars

little contrast between primaries and secondaries

Dusky-capped

Dusky-capped Flycatcher

Myiarchus tuberculifer

L 6.3–7.3″ (16.0–18.5 cm), WT 0.71 oz (20 g)

GENERAL IDENTIFICATION Dusky-capped Flycatcher is the smallest regularly occurring *Myiarchus* in our region. It is a shy woodland bird, perching or foraging at all levels, from just above the ground up to the canopy, often within vegetation rather than out in the open. Two subspecies occur in our region. The regularly occurring subspecies in Arizona and California is *M. t. olivascens*; *M. t. lawrenceii* occurs along the Caribbean slope of Mexico and Central America and is vagrant to southern and coastal Texas.

Dusky-capped has a slender build and relatively thin bill with a straight culmen. It has a proportionately long and narrow tail, which accentuates its slender appearance. Dusky-capped's tail often narrows toward the body. Its primary projection is relatively short. Its crown tends to be round, though occasionally it is slightly peaked. The crown, nape, mantle, and face are dark brown/gray (*lawrenceii* is darker above than *olivascens*). The chin and throat are medium gray, and the belly is medium yellow. The crown and face are similarly dark, contrasting with a slightly lighter gray throat and chest, which in turn contrast with the yellow belly. The wingbars are dull and similar in color to the mantle, rarely standing out (wingbars in juveniles or in adult *lawrenceii* can be more rufous). Unlike other *Myiarchus* flycatchers, which have whitish secondary feather edges, Dusky-capped's secondaries (except for the tertials) and primaries all have rufous or yellowish edges, resulting in weak wing panel contrast. Weak wing panel contrast characterizes *lawrenceii* as well, but the secondary and primary feather edges tend to be brighter rufous than *olivascens*. In both subspecies, the underside of the folded tail shows limited to no rufous, often appearing dark altogether (although in *lawrenceii*, rufous in folded tail may be more evident). Prebasic molt commences on summering grounds but completes (flight feathers) on wintering grounds.

VOCALIZATIONS Dusky-capped's characteristic call is a mournful drawn-out whistled "*peeEEeew*," rising and then descending (reminiscent of a wood-pewee). No other *Myiarchus* flycatchers in our region gives this type of call. Other Dusky-capped calls include a short rising "*whit*," and a rapid somewhat burry series, "*tee-teerrrrrrrr-deew*," often followed by a prolonged twitter. The latter is often given when it is agitated. Its song incorporates various combinations of call notes into a long series, "*peeew-tr-tr-drrr*" ("look, I'm here"), repeated over and over. It calls or sings frequently at dawn, although the mournful "*peeEEeew*" call can often be heard during the day, usually deep in woodland. Differences between *olivascens* and *lawrenceii* vocalizations are subtle, but "*peeEEeew*" call notes of *lawrenceii* are slightly lower in frequency than those of *olivascens*.

HABITAT, DISTRIBUTION, AND SEASONAL STATUS Dusky-capped is primarily a subtropical to tropical bird, whose range extends from northern Mexico south into the upper Amazon in South America. For most of its range in Mexico and Central America it is resident. In our region, it is mostly only a summer resident with a range restricted to the mountains of southeastern Arizona and southwestern New Mexico (common) and west Texas (rare). It prefers mixed pine-oak and sycamore-lined riparian woodlands in mountains and foothills. Breeding birds arrive in Arizona in late Mar., with most returning to Mexico by the end of Aug. (some stragglers may remain into Oct.). It is mostly absent from the United States in winter, but it is a regular vagrant to coastal California in late fall (a few have been recorded in coastal Oregon and Washington), with some overwintering (early Nov. to late Mar.). It is a very rare late fall and winter vagrant to southern Texas and along the Gulf Coast. Vagrants are usually found in wooded areas, including suburban parks.

Breeding birds in Arizona and Texas, as well as vagrants to the Pacific coast, are of the western Mexican *olivascens* subspecies. Vagrants to southern Texas and the Gulf of Mexico coast are of the more brightly colored *lawrenceii* subspecies. Many other subspecies of Dusky-capped exist further south and into South America, but it is unlikely these subspecies wander to the United States.

SIMILAR SPECIES Dusky-capped differs from most other *Myiarchus* by its small and slender body, thinner bill, and proportionately longer and narrower tail. Dusky-capped is most likely to be confused with Nutting's and Ash-throated, which are only slightly larger. Dusky-capped, however, is much darker above and brighter yellow below than Ash-throated. The wingbars of Dusky-capped are dull, whereas Ash-throated and Nutting's have paler wingbars that stand out more against their mantles and wings. The limited rufous in Dusky-capped's tail when seen from below is generally diagnostic. Dusky-capped's face and crown are of similar darkness to Nutting's, but in Nutting's the face is slightly paler than its crown. Brown-crested is larger, bulkier, thicker billed, and has more rufous in the tail. Dusky-capped's narrow and long tail often narrows toward the body, whereas Brown-crested's tail does not usually narrow. Dusky-capped is the only *Myiarchus* to give whistled pewee-like calls.

DUSKY-CAPPED FLYCATCHER

dark cap and face contrast with gray throat

crown peaked or rounded

olivascens

thin bill with relatively straight culmen

low wing panel contrast

secondary and primary edges rufous

dull wingbars

bright yellow

rusty wingbars

lawrenceii

relatively strong contrast and transition between gray chest and yellow belly

tail sometimes narrows at base

undertail appears mostly dark

less rufous on upperside of tail

undertails

comparison of underside of bills

slightly broader base

Dusky-capped

Nutting's

Ash-throated

cooperi

magister

Dusky-capped

Ash-throated

Brown-crested

DUSKY-CAPPED FLYCATCHER

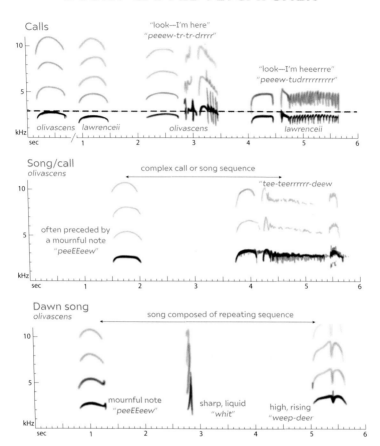

Calls

"look—I'm here"
"peeew-tr-tr-drrrr"

"look—I'm heeerrre"
"peeew-tudrrrrrrrrrr"

olivascens lawrenceii   olivascens   lawrenceii

Song/call
olivascens

complex call or song sequence

"tee-teerrrrrr-deew

often preceded by
a mournful note
"peeEEeew"

Dawn song
olivascens

song composed of repeating sequence

mournful note
"peeEEeew"

sharp, liquid
"whit"

high, rising
"weep-deer

DUSKY-CAPPED FLYCATCHER

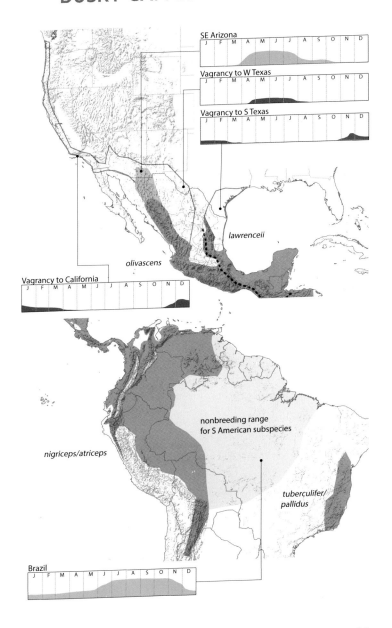

SE Arizona
J F M A M J J A S O N D

Vagrancy to W Texas
J F M A M J J A S O N D

Vagrancy to S Texas
J F M A M J J A S O N D

lawrenceii

olivascens

Vagrancy to California
J F M A M J J A S O N D

nonbreeding range
for S American subspecies

nigriceps/atriceps

*tuberculifer/
pallidus*

Brazil
J F M A M J J A S O N D

Ash-throated Flycatcher

Myiarchus cinerascens

L 7.5–8.5″ (19.0–21.6 cm), WT 0.75–1.31 oz (21.2–37.0 g)

GENERAL IDENTIFICATION The Ash-throated Flycatcher is a common summer resident of open woodlands, scrublands, and riparian areas of the western United States. During the breeding season, it frequently perches on and calls from the tops of bushes or trees. It is a medium-sized *Myiarchus* with a medium-sized bill. Its primary projection is variable but generally short, and its tail is relatively long. The bill is usually completely dark, but occasionally shows a pale base. The mouth lining, only seen when the bird opens its mouth, is yellowish or flesh-colored. Overall, Ash-throated is the palest of the regularly occurring North American *Myiarchus* flycatchers. It has a light gray to brown crown and mantle, and a pale gray throat and upper chest that grades gradually to a pale yellow belly. The pale throat shows weak contrast with its gray crown and pale yellow belly. The wing ground color ranges from medium brown to darkish brown, only slightly darker than the gray-brown mantle. The wingbars and tertial edges are whitish, but because the mantle and wing ground color are not dark, the wingbars and tertial edges show weak to medium contrast with the wings and mantle. The primary feather edges are conspicuously edged with rufous, but the secondary edges are usually uniformly whitish or very pale yellow (except for juveniles, which may have uniform rufous-edged secondaries), resulting in a strong wing panel contrast. The underside of the tail shows extensive rufous. Unique to *Myiarchus* is that the underside of the adult tail displays a narrow brown outer margin (confined to the outer webs of the tail feathers), which gradually increases in width toward the tip of the tail (bleeding over to the inner web of the tail feather), and then hooks strongly inward at the tip of the tail. On the folded tail, the dark hooking often extends across the tip of the tail, generating a dark terminal band across the tip of the folded undertail. Beware of juvenal plumaged birds. The extent of terminal hooking, unfortunately, is highly reduced in juvenal plumage (Aug. to Nov.). Juvenal secondary feather edges can also be extensively rufous instead of white, resulting in weak wing panel contrast. The prebasic molt begins on summering grounds but is mostly completed on migratory stopover sites in southwestern United States or on wintering grounds, so adults look worn in late summer. First-year birds, however, look fresh in late summer/early fall.

VOCALIZATIONS Ash-throated gives a distinct two-syllable call, which can be heard from afar. These include a frequent "*chi-keerrr*" call, with the last syllable having a burry descending quality (recalling a referee's whistle) and a shorter "*chi-krrr?*" or "*chi-up?*" call with the last syllable rising (the latter mostly given during the breeding season). Other less diagnostic calls include a sharp "*kwip*" (often given in quick succession) or soft "*prrt*" (frequently given in fall and winter). The song is a series that combines different call notes and their variations, "*KWIP-prr-drr-dr*," given frequently at dawn. The songs are often interspersed with isolated call notes, particularly the "*chi-keerrr*" or "*chi-krrr?*" call.

HABITAT, DISTRIBUTION, AND SEASONAL STATUS Ash-throated is the only common *Myiarchus* flycatcher in the western United States outside the desert southwest. It is a bird of open woodlands, dry scrub, chaparral, and riparian edges from sea level into the foothills and mid-elevations of mountains. It is generally absent from pure coniferous forests. Where its range overlaps with Brown-crested's, it inhabits more open and drier habitats, whereas Brown-crested prefers riparian habitats and edges.

In North America, it is primarily a summer resident from Texas, Arizona, and California north to eastern Washington, Idaho, and interior basins in southern British Columbia. Breeding birds arrive in late Mar. in southern California, Arizona, and Texas, and in mid-Apr. in eastern Washington. Birds mostly depart breeding grounds by mid-July and are evident in desert oasis migrant traps by early Aug. Wintering birds arrive in central Mexico by Sept. It is a year-round resident in northern Mexico. Small numbers regularly winter in southern Arizona and western and central Texas, and along the Gulf of Mexico coast east to Florida. It is a rare but regular fall vagrant throughout the United States, particularly along the Atlantic coast, peaking in Nov.

SIMILAR SPECIES Adult Ash-throated's undertail pattern (dark brown across the tail tip) is unique and usually sufficient to distinguish it from other *Myiarchus* if seen well (see variability in Nutting's Flycatcher as well as variability in juvenile Ash-throated). When the undertail pattern is not seen and vocalizations not heard, great care is needed for identification. Ash-throated is most like Brown-crested and Nutting's. In Arizona, the *M. t. magister* subspecies of Brown-crested is usually separable based on structure: larger size, bulkier body, and thicker and longer bill. The slightly smaller *M. t. cooperi* subspecies of Brown-crested in south Texas approaches Ash-throated in size and bill shape, so caution is warranted. Brown-crested of both subspecies, however, tends to be brighter yellow below. The undertail pattern in adults is almost always diagnostic for separating these two species. Pay attention to secondary feather edges. In both species, secondary feather edges are pale, but in Brown-crested, the outermost secondary feather (s1) is often rufous (lowest feather in the folded secondary stack) instead of white as in adult Ash-throated.

Nutting's is intermediate between Dusky-capped and Ash-throated in most features and is thus a notorious identification challenge. Nutting's, however, has a slightly darker crown, face, and mantle, which contrasts more with the pale chest than is seen in Ash-throated. Nutting's crown is usually rounder than that of Ash-throated. Nutting's bill is also subtly smaller and thicker than the bill of Ash-throated. Collectively, these plumage and structural features give Nutting's a slightly cuter look than Ash-throated. The color of secondary feather edges should be scrutinized. The secondary edges in Nutting's grade from rufous in the outermost secondaries to pale yellow, whereas in adult Ash-throated, the outermost secondaries are generally uniform in color (beware of juvenal Ash-throated, in which nearly all secondary feather edges can be rufous). The dark outer margin to the outer-tail feather tends to hook more at the tip in Ash-throated, giving Ash-throated a dark band across the tip of the tail (as seen from underside). Nutting's is also a more secretive bird than Ash-throated, preferring shrubby thickets. Ash-throated's call notes often have a burry quality. Finally, the color of the mouth lining may be useful as the mouth lining of Nutting's is orange while Ash-throated's is yellow or flesh-colored.

Dusky-capped has a darker chest and throat, brighter yellow underparts, inconspicuous wingbars, darker upperparts, rufous edges to the secondaries, and limited rufous in the tail when seen from the underside. Ash-throated is distinguished from Great Crested by less contrasty appearance. Great Crested has dark gray chest, sharply demarcated from brighter yellow underparts, whereas Ash-throated's chest is a lighter gray that extends further down the chest, grading into the pale yellow belly. La Sagra's pale plumage is like Ash-throated's, but La Sagra's has a smaller body, longer and thinner bill, limited rufous in its tail, and whiter underparts.

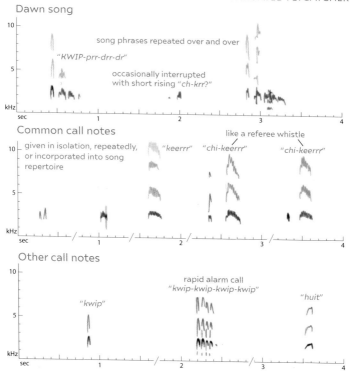

Dawn song

song phrases repeated over and over

"KWIP-prr-drr-dr"

occasionally interrupted
with short rising *"ch-krr?"*

Common call notes

given in isolation, repeatedly,
or incorporated into song
repertoire

"keerrr"

like a referee whistle

"chi-keerrr"

"chi-keerrr"

Other call notes

"kwip"

rapid alarm call
"kwip-kwip-kwip-kwip"

"huit"

ASH-THROATED FLYCATCHER

medium-sized bill

pale wingbars contrast weakly
with wings and mantle

low contrast

secondary panel in adults
with uniform white
edges

primary panel
with rufous edges

juvenile; note
secondary panel
may be rufous-edged

juvenile may also have noticeable
pale base to bill

dark wraps
around tip
of tail

Comparison and variation in undertail patterns of similar species
note juvs typically have more rufous than ads

ad   juv

Ash-throated
outer tail
feather R6

Ash-throated

Dusky-capped

Brown-crested

ASH-THROATED FLYCATCHER

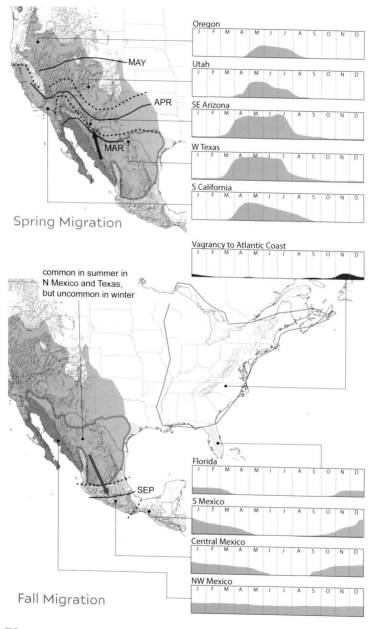

MAY

APR

MAR

Oregon

Utah

SE Arizona

W Texas

S California

Spring Migration

Vagrancy to Atlantic Coast

common in summer in
N Mexico and Texas,
but uncommon in winter

SEP

Florida

S Mexico

Central Mexico

NW Mexico

Fall Migration

Nutting's Flycatcher

Myiarchus nuttingi

L 7.1–7.5″ (18.0–19.1 cm); WT 0.74–0.84 oz (21.0–23.9 g)

GENERAL IDENTIFICATION Nutting's Flycatcher is primarily a bird of dry forests. It is easy to overlook because it is remarkably like Ash-throated in terms of structure and plumage, and because it is relatively shy, preferring to forage within vegetation than from exposed branches. Nutting's is probably best described as having characters intermediate between Dusky-capped and Ash-throated. It is a medium-sized *Myiarchus* with a medium-sized bill. It is slimmer than Ash-throated, but more robust than Dusky-capped. Primary projection is short. The crown of Nutting's tends to be rounded, unlike the more crested crowns of the larger *Myiarchus*. Its crown, mantle and face are dull brown, showing some contrast with pale gray throat and chest. The belly is dull yellow, brighter than in Ash-throated and lighter than in Great Crested, but like that of Brown-crested. Pay attention to the secondary wing panel's color patterns. The secondary feather edges grade from yellow to white from the outer secondaries inward, resulting in a secondary wing panel showing a gradual upward transition (toward inner secondaries) from yellow to whitish toward the tertials on the folded wing. The underside of the tail is rufous with a narrow brown outer margin that gradually widens toward the tip but does not hook or wrap completely around the tail tip as in Ash-throated. The wingbars are grayish and show only moderate contrast with wing and mantle.

VOCALIZATIONS Nutting's gives a rising "*weeep*" or "*weeEET*" call reminiscent of Great Crested, but slightly lower in frequency. Other distinctive calls include a clear, whistled "*hooit*," a liquid "*whit*," a squeaky "*wip-dit*," and flat "*peek*" calls, often given together in slow progression. It also gives squeaky chattering "*ch-ch-ch*" and a loud "*ka-bik*" call series. Its song, often given at dawn, is a series consisting of a variety of call notes followed by a gurgled or rolling ending.

HABITAT, DISTRIBUTION, AND SEASONAL STATUS Nutting's Flycatcher is primarily a non-migratory resident of arid subtropical to tropical forests and scrublands from northwestern Mexico south to northwestern Costa Rica. It is fond of semi-open environments with a scattering of dense shrubbery. Although resident throughout most of its range, small numbers wander north to Arizona and very rarely elsewhere (e.g., western Texas and California). Most of these wanderers seem to turn up in late fall (Nov.), staying through the winter, often around riparian habitats. However, in Arizona it may be a very rare but regular breeder.

SIMILAR SPECIES Nutting's is intermediate between Dusky-capped and Ash-throated in terms of structure and plumage. Sometimes a brightly colored, slightly small Ash-throated turns out to be a Nutting's, or a Nutting's is initially misidentified as a pale Dusky-capped. Dusky-capped has limited rufous in the tail, duller wingbars (concolorous with mantle), brighter yellow underparts, and darker gray upperparts, chest, and throat. Dusky-capped also has a more slender body, a thinner and straighter bill, and a longer, narrower tail. Adult Ash-throated is overall paler and less contrasty than Nutting's. Ash-throated's face is generally paler gray than its crown, but in Nutting's the face and crown are both brown. The brown outer margin of Ash-throated's tail hooks across the tip of the tail, whereas the terminal hooking of Nutting's never cuts across the tip of the tail (but beware of juvenile Ash-throated, which may have limited terminal hooking). The edges of the secondary feathers on adult Ash-throated are of uniform color, whitish or pale yellow, resulting in a uniform secondary panel that contrasts with the rufous primary panel. In Nutting's, the secondary panel on the folded wing grades smoothly upward from yellow by the primaries to white toward the tertials.

However, be careful of immature Ash-throated, which can have more colorful, even rufous-edged, secondaries, but unlike the continuous gradation across secondaries in Nutting's, most of the secondary edges in juvenal Ash-throated are uniformly rufous. Nutting's also tends to have a rounder crown than Ash-throated. The bill of Nutting's is slightly shorter and proportionately thicker than Ash-throated's. The lining of Nutting's mouth is orange instead of the flesh-color or yellow of Ash-throated. The calls of Nutting's have a whistled quality, whereas Ash-throated's calls include burry components. Overall, Nutting's has a slightly cuter look than Ash-throated.

NUTTING'S FLYCATCHER

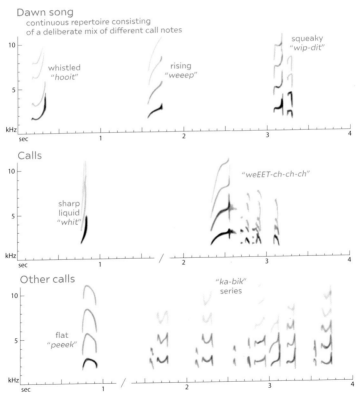

79

Dusky-capped has a darker crown, chest, and face; a thinner bill with a straighter culmen; weak wingbar contrast; a longer and narrower tail; and limited to no rufous on the undertail. In terms of overall plumage patterns and colors, Brown-crested is like Nutting's, but structurally it is a larger, bulkier bird with a larger and thicker bill: a Nutting's on steroids.

NUTTING'S FLYCATCHER

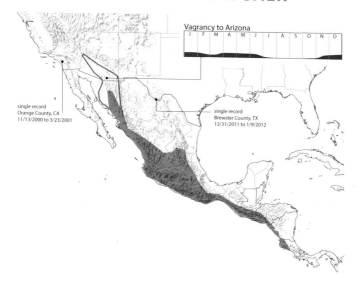

Vagrancy to Arizona

J F M A M J J A S O N D

single record
Orange County, CA
11/13/2000 to 3/23/2001

single record
Brewster County, TX
12/31/2011 to 1/9/2012

NUTTING'S FLYCATCHER

crown slightly rounded

low contrast between cheek and crown

secondary panel transitions from rufous to yellowish CARE needed (see juv Ash-throated plate)

short primary projection

medium contrast between cheek and throat

brown cheek

yellowish underparts, brighter than Ash-throated

rufous undertail with limited dark tip BEWARE juv Ash-throated

mouth lining on Nutting's orange vs flesh-colored or yellowish on Ash-throated

Nutting's

Ash-throated

Nutting's averages shorter primary projection than Ash-throated, but there is overlap

Ash-throated

Nutting's

Dusky-capped

Brown-crested

Great Crested Flycatcher

Myiarchus crinitus

L 6.7–8.3″ (17.0–21.1 cm), WT 0.96–1.40 oz (27.2–39.6 g)

GENERAL IDENTIFICATION The Great Crested Flycatcher is a
common spring and summer resident of the eastern hardwood
forests of the United States. Although not a secretive bird, its habit
of sitting motionless high up in the shade of the forest canopy often
makes it difficult to find. However, its loud and distinctive call
usually gives away its presence. Great Crested has a dark gray-brown
head, face, and mantle along with a dark gray chest. The mantle often
shows a green tint, and this is unique among *Myiarchus* species.
The underparts are uniform lemon yellow from the undertail
coverts to the base of the dark gray upper chest. There is a weak
contrast between the dark upper chest and dark upperparts, but
the contrast between the dark gray chest and yellow underparts is
strong, accentuated by a sharp demarcation between the gray and
yellow. These features give Great Crested a hooded appearance. The
demarcation between the gray chest and yellow underparts is higher
up on the chest than in other *Myiarchus*. The lower rear of the eye is
often bordered by a thin, pale edge, a mere fragment of an eye-ring,
but because of the dark face it tends to stand out. This feature is less
often seen in other *Myiarchus*.

   As for most *Myiarchus*, the greater and median covert feathers and
the flight feathers have pale edges, but because the ground color of the
wing feathers is dark, Great Crested typically has a contrasting wing
pattern with whitish wingbars and contrasting whitish edges to the
tertials (innermost secondaries). The whitish tertial edges in Great
Crested are typically white, accentuating the contrasting wing pattern.
Unique to Great Crested (in fresh birds) is that the white edge of
the innermost secondary (e.g., s9 or top tertial on folded wing) is
distinctly broader than the pale edges on the other tertials (s8 and s7),
making the s9 tertial edge very conspicuous (in other *Myiarchus*, the

widths of tertial edges are similar). The wingbars and whitish tertial edges are brighter than the mantle, whereas the wing ground color is darker than the mantle. The primary feathers have rufous edges. The outer secondaries (often hidden by the tertials on a folded wing) have pale rufous or yellow edges. The rufous-edged primaries contrast with the white-edged tertials. Note that juvenile birds often have extensive rufous on secondaries. The tail pattern is distinctive: From above, the central tail feathers are dark like the wing ground color, often contrasting with the brown upperparts. The inner web of outer-tail feathers is bright rufous, such that when seen from below or in flight, the undertail is extensively rufous. The outer web of outer-tail feathers is dark brown; from below, the tail is rufous with a straight, narrow brown outer-tail margin of uniform width. Unlike in other *Myiarchus*, the dark coloration in the outer-tail feather is usually confined to the outer web and does not bleed over to the inner web.

Structurally, Great Crested is a large, big-headed *Myiarchus*. It has the longest primary projection of all *Myiarchus*, because it is a long-distance migrant. Because of its slightly longer wings, its tail appears slightly shorter than that of other *Myiarchus*. Its tail is relatively wide and rarely narrows toward the body. The bill is medium sized, often with a pale base, especially in juveniles.

The prebasic molt is usually completed on summering grounds or along coastal stopovers (although sometimes completed on wintering grounds), so adult Great Cresteds can often appear fresh like first-year birds in fall.

VOCALIZATIONS Great Crested gives a very distinctive rising "*weep*" call, sometimes terminating with an abrupt downward inflection, "*weep-a*." This call is given throughout the day and can often be heard from deep within the forest. It frequently gives a burry monotonic "*brrrt*" call, reminiscent of the call of a Red-headed Woodpecker (*Melanerpes erythrocephalus*). When agitated, it can give a short burst of rising "*brrreet*" calls, often repeated in succession. It also gives a liquid "*hooit*" call and a short, somewhat low and hollow-sounding "*kwip*" call, sometimes in rapid succession. Its song consists of a slow and continuous succession of rising "*weep*" notes, burry "*brrt*" notes, and other call notes.

HABITAT, DISTRIBUTION, AND SEASONAL STATUS The Great Crested Flycatcher is a summer bird of the deciduous forests of eastern North America, from the Gulf of Mexico coast north to southeastern Canada and Alberta. It winters from southern Mexico through Central America to Colombia. The Great Crested requires forested areas with tall trees, but within these areas, it frequents more open areas, such as forest edges, clearings, riparian areas, and shady suburban habitats. Its nests are in secondary cavities (e.g., woodpecker holes) lined with various twigs and fibers, often with snake skin at the nest opening.

Great Crested is a long-distance migrant. In spring, migrants pass through the United States between mid-Mar. and late May. On its southerly nesting grounds (e.g., Gulf Coast), it arrives in mid-Mar. On its northerly nesting grounds (e.g., Minnesota), it arrives in early May. Birds begin departing their breeding grounds in July and are nearly all gone by late Aug. Fall migrants pass through southern Texas between mid-Aug. and early Oct., peaking in mid-Sept. The first migrants arrive on wintering grounds in southern Mexico in early Sept. and in Colombia in early Oct.

Spring migrants take a western circum-Gulf of Mexico route through Texas or a trans-Gulf route between the Yucatan and eastern Texas/Louisiana before spreading out across eastern North America. Fall migrants predominantly follow the western circum-Gulf of Mexico route. A few migrants cross the Caribbean and into Florida. Small numbers can be found in southern Florida at all times of the year.

Great Crested is a rare vagrant to the west, mostly along the Pacific coast, especially in California. Vagrant records overwhelmingly fall between the second week of Sept. and the third week of Oct., peaking from late Sept. to early Oct. Outside of Florida, it is largely absent from the United States during the winter, although there are a few remarkable winter records that may pertain to lingering fall vagrants.

SIMILAR SPECIES Great Crested is most like Brown-crested and Ash-throated Flycatchers, but it is a much more colorful bird, showing significant plumage contrast. The border between Great Crested's dark gray chest and bright yellow underparts is strongly demarcated, resulting in strong contrast between the gray upper chest and yellow belly. This feature alone is often sufficient to distinguish it from other *Myiarchus* flycatchers. Other features that can be indicative of Great Crested are its pale bill base, blackish ground color to wings, bold white tertial edges, relatively bold wingbars, and contrasting pale border to the lower rear of the eye. Ash-throated and Brown-crested have pale gray chests and throats that grade gradually into light yellow underparts. Bright Brown-crested is like dull Great Crested in terms of color, but Great Crested has darker upperparts and has a more contrasty plumage. The wingbars and tertial edges on Ash-throated and Brown-crested are duller than in Great Crested. The brown outer-tail margin on Ash-throated hooks inward across the tail tip. The brown outer-tail margin on Brown-crested is wider than on Great Crested. The primary projections in other *Myiarchus* flycatchers are generally shorter than in Great Crested, but be sure to assess primary projection relative to the *longest* tertial. La Sagra's and Dusky-capped have limited rufous in the tail. Dusky-capped's dark chest is like that of Great Crested, but Dusky-capped is a slimmer bird with a smaller and thinner bill. Great Crested's rising "*weep*" calls are usually diagnostic.

GREAT CRESTED FLYCATCHER

pale base to bill

medium-sized bill

strong wing panel contrast

white edges to secondaries

dark gray chest

bright yellow belly

rufous primaries

hooded appearance

often streaky gray border to upper breast

underside of bills

more extensively pink lower mandible

Ash-throated   Brown-crested   Great Crested

contrasting wingbars

generally longer primary projection

extensive rufous undertail

strong contrast between chest and belly

often shows contrasting pale area below eye (rear)

broad white edge to uppermost tertial

NOTE thinner white edge in worn birds

worn birds may show less broad white edge

white edge not as broad and not significantly broader than feathers below

Tertials

broad white edge

bright white tertials

juvs show rufous secondaries

Great Crested   Ash-throated   Brown-crested

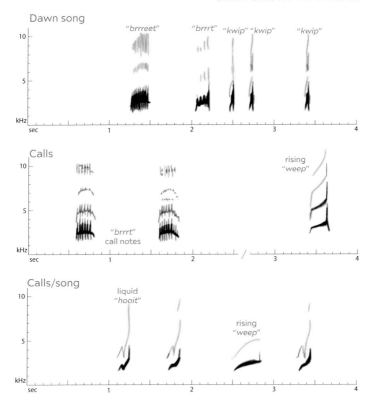

Dawn song

"brrreet"   "brrrt" "kwip" "kwip"   "kwip"

Calls

rising "weep"

"brrrt" call notes

Calls/song

liquid "hooit"

rising "weep"

GREAT CRESTED FLYCATCHER

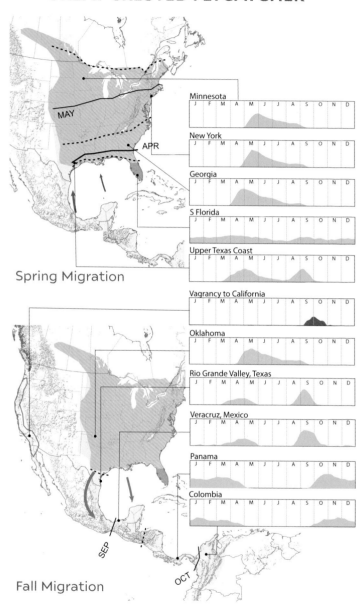

Minnesota

New York

Georgia

S Florida

Upper Texas Coast

Spring Migration

Vagrancy to California

Oklahoma

Rio Grande Valley, Texas

Veracruz, Mexico

Panama

Colombia

Fall Migration

MAY

APR

SEP

OCT

Brown-crested Flycatcher

Myiarchus tyrannulus

L 7.1–9.1″ (18.0–23.1 cm)

WT *M. t. magister* 1.28–1.85 oz (36.4–52.5 g)
M. t. cooperi 1.08–1.59 oz (30.7–45.0 g)

GENERAL IDENTIFICATION The Brown-crested Flycatcher is
the largest *Myiarchus* in our region. It can often be found sitting
in or at the tops of shrubs, trees, and tall cacti, such as saguaros.
It has a largish head and a long, thick bill. Brown-crested has a
medium-brown mantle and crown. Its face and nape are medium
gray. In good light, the subtle contrast between the brown crown
and the gray face may be apparent. Its throat and chest are pale gray,
transitioning gradually into a yellowish belly. Overall, the intensity
of yellow on the belly is intermediate between Ash-throated (pale
yellow) and Great Crested (bright yellow). Its gray chest and throat
contrast moderately with a brownish crown and yellowish belly. In
Brown-crested there is a tendency for the edge of the outermost
secondary feather (s1) to be rufous, with other secondary edges
being white. Thus, on a folded wing, the lower part (s1) of the
secondary panel appears rufous and transitions abruptly upward to
white (s2 to s9). This feature is not generally seen in other *Myiarchus*,
but more study on this feature is needed. Brown-crested's tail is
extensively rufous on the underside, but it displays a straight, brown
outer margin of uniform width. However, the brown outer margin is
wider than that of Great Crested because it bleeds into the inner web.
Brown-crested's wingbars are light gray and moderately stand out
from the wing and mantle.

Two subspecies exist in our region, the smaller *M. t. cooperi* of
southern Texas and eastern Mexico and the larger *M. t. magister* of
Arizona and western Mexico. Plumages are nearly identical, but the
larger *magister* has a proportionately longer bill than *cooperi*. The

prebasic molt commences on summering grounds and completes (flight feathers) on wintering grounds.

VOCALIZATIONS Brown-crested calls include a variety of short burry "*brrr*" or "*brrt*" notes (rising or descending), a liquid rising "*whit*," and a short "*pip*" (often repeated in rapid succession). It also gives short chortling "*brr-dip*" and "*brrp*" calls, and slow twitters. Its songs consist of a series of alternating burry notes, "*brEEer—tu-tudrr*" or "*hooET—tu-tudrr*" with distinct undulations in frequency, giving its song a rolling quality. These burry song phrases are often repeated persistently, especially at dawn. Single "*whit*" or "*pip*" notes are often interjected between these song phrases.

HABITAT, DISTRIBUTION, AND SEASONAL STATUS Brown-crested can be found in a wide variety of habitats. In our region, its range is restricted to the arid environments of the southwestern United States and southern Texas. Within these environments, it can be found in mature riparian habitats, giant cactus forests, thorn scrub woodlands (acacia), oak woodlands, and mixed pine-oak woodlands. It is a secondary cavity nester and thus requires habitats with enough trees and woodpeckers for nesting sites. Where its range overlaps with Great Crested in central Texas, Brown-crested associates more with species of trees native to western areas (e.g., acacia), whereas Great Crested associates with eastern hardwood tree species, such as pecans and Bald Cypress (*Taxodium distichum*).

Brown-crested is generally a permanent resident from northern Mexico to Central America. In our region, it occurs primarily in the spring and summer, when northern Mexican birds move north. Birds arrive in Sonora (Mexico) and southeastern Arizona in mid-Apr. and quickly spread to northwestern Arizona and the Mojave Desert region of California. In southern Texas, birds arrive during the third week of Mar., ranging north up to the edge of the Edwards Plateau in central Texas. Most birds return south to Mexico by the end of July. Brown-crested shows relatively limited vagrancy, perhaps due to its adherence to wooded areas of arid environments. For example, in California, Brown-crested is rare along the coastal slope (or anywhere west of the Transverse Ranges) despite being relatively common in the Mojave Desert. In Texas, Brown-crested is common in the more arid shrublands of south Texas, but becomes very rare in the more humid and forested parts of eastern Texas. Nevertheless, Brown-crested is a rare but regular winter visitor to the Gulf of Mexico coast, particularly in southeastern Louisiana and southern Florida. Vagrants have turned up in northern California but in much smaller numbers than Dusky-capped and Great Crested.

Globally, there are seven currently recognized subspecies of Brown-crested, but only two in our region. California and Arizona birds are represented by the larger *magister* subspecies, whose range extends along the Pacific slope of Mexico south to Oaxaca, Mexico. Southern Texas birds are represented by *cooperi*, whose range extends along the Caribbean slope of eastern Mexico south to Honduras. The other Brown-crested subspecies are found in South America, with populations in Colombia and a migratory population in Brazil. South American subspecies are not known to occur as vagrants to the United States.

SIMILAR SPECIES In terms of plumage color intensity and contrast, Brown-crested is intermediate between Ash-throated and Great Crested. It is distinguished from Ash-throated by its larger bill, slightly brighter yellow underparts, slightly more contrasty face, grayer chest, and straight brown outer margin to tail (no hooking of brown outer web at tail tip as in Ash-throated). In the west, Brown-crested should also be noticeably larger, bulkier, and longer-billed than Ash-throated. It is distinguished from Great Crested by overall paler appearance, larger bill, less contrasting wingbars, and slightly wider dark outer margins on the folded undertail. Great Crested also has a longer primary projection, and a brighter and broader white edge to the innermost tertial. Note that in southern Texas Brown-crested (*cooperi*) is slightly smaller than in Arizona (*magister*) and can be similar in size as Great Crested. Dusky-capped is always smaller and darker overall with a small and thin bill, and limited rufous in the tail. Nutting's is similar in terms of plumage contrasts and brightness, but it is smaller in size and smaller bill, and has brighter yellow underparts.

Brown-crested's single "*kwip*" and "*brrr*" call notes are very similar to those of Ash-throated but are slightly lower in frequency. The more complex calls of Ash-throated and Brown-crested are easier to differentiate. Ash-throated typically gives two-syllable calls ("*chi-keer*" or "*chi-up*") with burry qualities restricted to the second syllable. Brown-crested's calls tend to be short, one-syllable burrs. Brown-crested's song is more undulating in frequency (giving it a rolling quality) and of slightly lower frequency than Ash-throated's, which is more monotonic and higher frequency.

BROWN-CRESTED FLYCATCHER

brown crown in good light

gray face

bulky body

gray throat

white edges to
secondaries

medium contrast

short primary
projection

rufous primaries

extensive rufous
in tail; narrow brown
margin to outer web usually
bleeds on to inner web

magister

underside of bill

cooperi

underside of bill

Dawn song

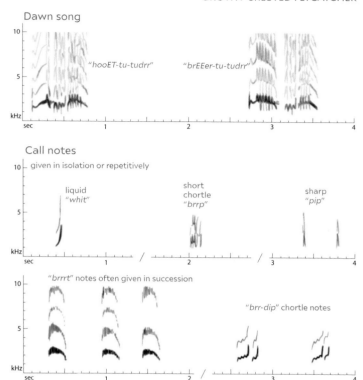

"hooET-tu-tudrr"   "brEEer-tu-tudrr"

Call notes

given in isolation or repetitively

liquid "whit"

short chortle "brrp"

sharp "pip"

"brrrt" notes often given in succession

"brr-dip" chortle notes

BROWN-CRESTED FLYCATCHER

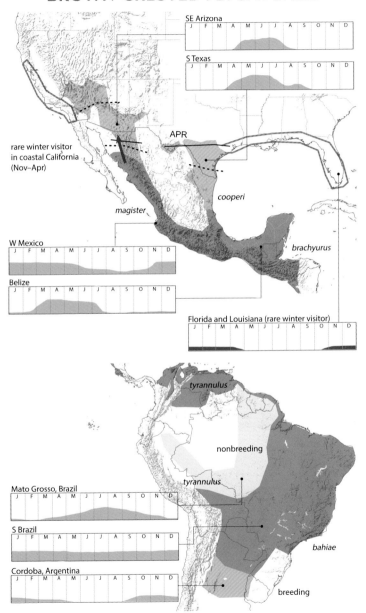

SE Arizona
J F M A M J J A S O N D

S Texas
J F M A M J J A S O N D

rare winter visitor
in coastal California
(Nov–Apr)

APR

cooperi

magister

brachyurus

W Mexico
J F M A M J J A S O N D

Belize
J F M A M J J A S O N D

Florida and Louisiana (rare winter visitor)
J F M A M J J A S O N D

tyrannulus

nonbreeding

tyrannulus

Mato Grosso, Brazil
J F M A M J J A S O N D

S Brazil
J F M A M J J A S O N D

Cordoba, Argentina
J F M A M J J A S O N D

bahiae

breeding

La Sagra's Flycatcher

Myiarchus sagrae

L 7.5–8.7" (19.1–22.1 cm)

WT *L. s. sagrae* 0.5–1.0 oz (14.2–28.4 g)

L. s. lucaysiensis 0.78 oz (22.0–22.3 g)

GENERAL IDENTIFICATION La Sagra's Flycatcher is a small *Myiarchus* of the Caribbean. Its appearance recalls Ash-throated Flycatcher, but it is much paler. La Sagra's is almost entirely pale below, with little to no yellow. It has a dark bushy crest. Its tail shows little rufous. Primaries have brown to rufous edges. Secondaries have light gray edges. The bill is medium in length, primary projection is short, and the tail is relatively long. La Sagra's frequently leans forward (at an angle of 45°) when perched.

VOCALIZATIONS La Sagra's call is a short rising "*peet*," shorter than the rising "*weep*" of Great Crested, but longer than the liquid "*whit*" of Dusky-capped and Brown-crested. Calls also include a sharp "*pip*," quick "*pip-pip*," and "*pitdr*" calls, sometimes repeated in rapid succession. Song consists of high-pitched "*pit—piDEeer*," recalling a kiskadee but much higher in frequency. The frequency of its song is higher than that of other *Myiarchus*, overlapping instead with the frequency range of some *Empidonax* flycatcher songs.

HABITAT, DISTRIBUTION, AND SEASONAL STATUS La Sagra's is primarily resident in Cuba and the Bahamas, where it can be found in a diversity of wooded habitats including pine forests, mixed woodlands, shrubby thickets, and mangroves. It is a secondary cavity nester. It is a rare but regular vagrant to the United States. Almost all records are from southeastern Florida, including the Florida Keys, with records in fall, winter, spring, and early summer. There are only two records of vagrants away from southeastern Florida: an individual from Sept. 14, 1963 in Orrville, Alabama, and another on Apr. 14–15, 2013 from Sarasota, Florida. It was previously considered conspecific with the Stolid Flycatcher (*M. stolidus*) of Jamaica and Hispaniola. Two subspecies of La Sagra's are recognized, with *L. s. sagrae* in Cuba and *L. s. lucaysiensis* in the Bahamas. Vagrants to Florida are most likely *lucaysiensis*. The Orrville, Alabama record may have been the nominate subspecies from Cuba.

SIMILAR SPECIES Due to its pale coloration, it is only likely to be confused with Ash-throated. However, note La Sagra's smaller size, longer and thinner bill, minimal rufous in tail, much paler chest and belly, and darker and often bushier crest. La Sagra's calls and songs are much higher in frequency than Ash-throated.

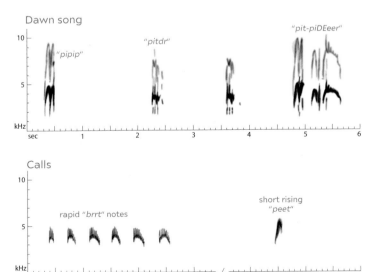

LA SAGRA'S FLYCATCHER

LA SAGRA'S FLYCATCHER

crown raised

often appears flat-headed
with crest down

small *Myiarchus* with
dark cap and plumage
similar to Eastern Phoebe

dull wingbars

dark cap

weak
contrast

very pale
below

lucaysiensis has
more rufous
in tail

quite a long
slender bill

very little
rufous in tail

LA SAGRA'S FLYCATCHER

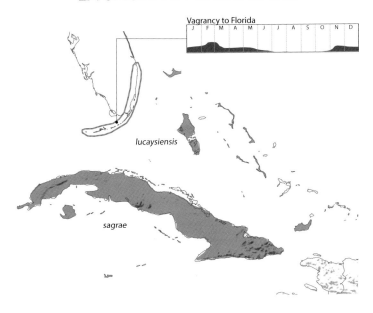

Vagrancy to Florida

| J | F | M | A | M | J | J | A | S | O | N | D |

lucaysiensis

sagrae

Kingbirds (*Tyrannus*)

Tyrannus (Kingbirds)
Identifying Tyrannus *kingbirds*

Kingbirds are large tyrant flycatchers, often with vivid or strongly contrasting plumages. They have large bills compared with other flycatchers like the *Empidonax*. They tend to perch in exposed areas, such as the tops of trees, dead snags, fences, and powerlines, and are often seen flycatching or pouncing on prey from these posts. Unlike *Empidonax* flycatchers and phoebes, they do not flick their wings or tails.

The kingbirds can be visually grouped into those with yellow bellies and those with whitish bellies. The **yellow-bellied kingbirds** include Tropical, Couch's, Cassin's, Thick-billed, and Western Kingbirds. The first step in identifying a Yellow-bellied Kingbird is to determine whether it is a Tropical/Couch's or a Cassin's/Western. The former has short primary projections and the latter long. Thick-billed Kingbird is usually straightforward to identify because of its pale belly, thick bill, and bulky body. Once a kingbird identification can be narrowed down, one can focus on the finer details of separating Tropical from Couch's and Cassin's from Western.

The **white-bellied kingbirds** include Eastern, Gray, and Loggerhead Kingbirds, and Scissor-tailed and Fork-tailed Flycatchers. Eastern, Gray, and Loggerhead Kingbirds can be superficially similar. Scissor-tailed and Fork-tailed Flycatchers are unmistakable, but confusion can occur with immature or molting birds, which can have shorter tails. Immature Fork-tailed can be confused with Eastern Kingbird, whereas immature Scissor-tailed can be confused with Western Kingbird.

On very rare occasions, kingbirds may hybridize, but their offspring are not viable. Hybrid examples will be discussed separately at the end of the species accounts.

Shape, size, and structure. Besides the obvious differences between those with long (Fork-tailed and Scissor-tailed Flycatchers) and short tails, pay attention to subtle differences in overall size and shape. Kingbirds range from slim to bulky in shape. There are also subtle differences in size and shape of bill. The yellow-bellied kingbirds, for example, are mostly similar in shape, but Thick-billed is short-tailed, short-winged, and bulky in size compared with the slenderer bodies of Western, Cassin's, Tropical, and Couch's. Tropical tends to be slightly slenderer than Couch's. Loggerhead, Thick-billed, and Gray Kingbirds have large bills. Eastern, Western, and Cassin's Kingbirds, and Fork-tailed and Scissor-tailed Flycatchers have medium-sized bills.

Wing shape, particularly the length of the outer primaries, differs between kingbird species. Western and Cassin's Kingbirds have long **primary projections** compared with Tropical and Couch's. Eastern has a long primary projection compared with Gray and Loggerhead.

With easy access to high-speed photography, today birders are afforded the ability to capture detailed images of spread wings in flight. Careful examination of the flight feathers can be useful in identification. For example, the long primary projections of Western and Cassin's Kingbirds give them more pointy wings, in which the outer primaries protrude well beyond the secondaries and inner primaries. The shorter primary projections in Tropical and Couch's result in more rounded wing tips, with the outer primaries protruding less for these two species compared with Western and Cassin's. The exact wing formula (especially the relative differences in the lengths of outer primaries) is often diagnostic of a particular species. Finally, the geometry of primary feather tips is useful for aging and sexing. Males have notched and highly attenuated outer primary tips (notching is less prominent in females). Juvenal outer primaries usually lack notching altogether.

SHAPE AND STRUCTURE

Thick-billed

Tropical

Cassin's

Loggerhead

PRIMARY PROJECTION

extreme birds are illustrated as there is some overlap

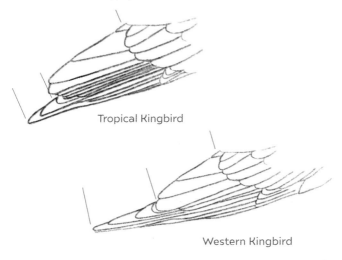

Tropical Kingbird

Western Kingbird

Cassin's adult male
notched
primaries

p10 ——
p9 ——

Cassin's juvenile

be careful when assessing as primary projection
appears longer with drooped wings

Plumage coloration and contrast. Relative color intensity and contrasts between parts of a bird's body should be studied. Focus on relative brightness and contrast between the upperparts and underparts, tail and mantle, wings and mantle, auriculars (ear patch) and face, chest and belly, head and mantle, and face and throat. Western and Cassin's have gray chests whereas Tropical and Couch's have more yellowish chests. Thick-billed has a white to pale lemon yellow chest. For Western and Cassin's, note the darkness of the chest and degree to which it contrasts with the throat. For Tropical and Couch's, brightness of yellow on the chest should be noted. Pay close attention to face patterns and contrast, comparing darkness of face and crown with the color of the chin and throat. Cassin's, Tropical, Couch's, and Thick-billed have dark crowns and often blackish ear patches that contrast with the rest of the face. Cassin's has a white chin that contrasts with the dark gray face and chest. Western also has a whitish chin, but the face is lighter gray so the contrast between chin and face is not as strong as in Cassin's. All adult kingbirds have yellow or red median crowns, but these are usually hidden. Consider yourself special if you see the concealed crown in the field.

HEAD CONTRAST

weak
(e.g., Western)

strong
(e.g., Cassin's)

BODY COLOR

whitish

Thick-billed Kingbird

gray

yellow

Cassin's Kingbird
Western Kingbird

black

white

Eastern Kingbird

Tail pattern and shape. Tails are usually dark, but note whether the tail has white outer margins (Western) or white tips (Cassin's). Note also whether the tip of the tail is forked (Tropical, Gray, and Couch's) or squarish (Western, Cassin's, and Eastern). Beware of the effects of feather wear and backlighting in perception of pale margins or tips to tail.

TAIL PATTERNS—UNDERSIDE

Kingbirds

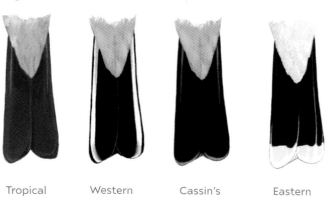

Tropical   Western   Cassin's   Eastern

Vocalizations. Each of these kingbirds has unique and diagnostic calls. Learn to distinguish "*pip*" from "*breer*" notes. Some give rapid twitters and others give squeaky calls, often repeated quickly in the form of a chatter. Western Kingbird, Couch's Kingbird, and Scissor-tailed Flycatcher give "*pip*" calls, but the other kingbirds do not. Most kingbirds twitter, but Couch's and Cassin's Kingbirds and Scissor-tailed Flycatcher do not twitter. Burry "*breEEer*" calls are given by Couch's, Cassin's, and Loggerhead Kingbirds, whereas buzzy, high-pitched calls are given by Eastern Kingbird. Rising "*chuEE*" calls are unique to Thick-billed Kingbird.

	Tropical Kingbird	Couch's Kingbird	Cassin's Kingbird	Western Kingbird	Thick-billed Kingbird	Eastern Kingbird	Gray Kingbird	Loggerhead Kingbird	Scissor-tailed Flycatcher	Fork-tailed Flycatcher
high pitch insect-like buzz "bzzew"						■				
"breEEer" "brrr"		■	■					■		
"chuEE"					■					
squeaky notes		■	■		■			■		
twitters	■			■	■		■	■		■
"pip"		■					■		■	

sec   1

The "yellow-bellied" kingbirds

KINGBIRD COMPARISON

shorter, stouter bill than Tropical

bright yellow breast contrasts with white throat

long bill

brighter green back than Western

dull green breast

brownish forked tail

browner wings than Western

shorter primaries than Western

Couch's

dark brown forked tail

Tropical

light gray chest

dull wingbars

longer pointed primaries than Tropical/Couch's

grayish-green chest

more contrasting black tail than Tropical/Couch's

stronger wingbars

Western

pale tips to dark brown tail

white does not extend past eye

Cassin's

KINGBIRD COMPARISON

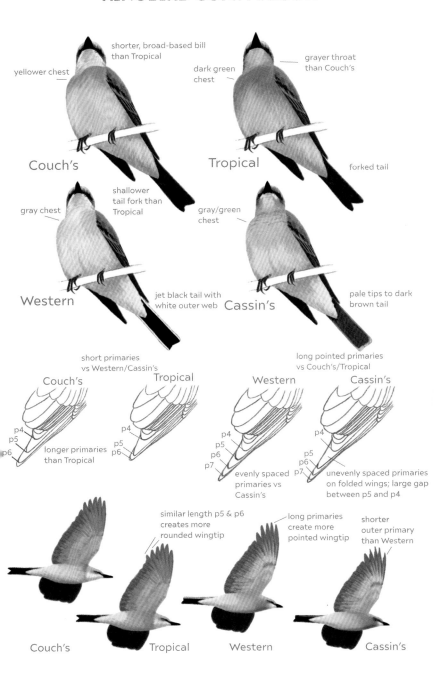

shorter, broad-based bill than Tropical

yellower chest

Couch's

grayer throat than Couch's

dark green chest

Tropical

forked tail

shallower tail fork than Tropical

gray chest

Western

jet black tail with white outer web

gray/green chest

Cassin's

pale tips to dark brown tail

short primaries vs Western/Cassin's

Couch's

Tropical

longer primaries than Tropical

p4
p5
p6

p4
p5
p6

long pointed primaries vs Couch's/Tropical

Western

Cassin's

p4
p5
p6
p7

evenly spaced primaries vs Cassin's

p4
p5
p6
p7

unevenly spaced primaries on folded wings; large gap between p5 and p4

similar length p5 & p6 creates more rounded wingtip

long primaries create more pointed wingtip

shorter outer primary than Western

Couch's

Tropical

Western

Cassin's

YELLOW-BELLIED KINGBIRDS IN FLIGHT

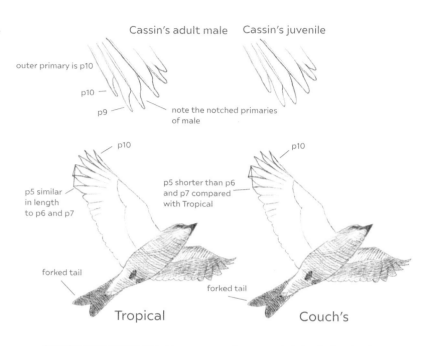

Cassin's adult male

Cassin's juvenile

outer primary is p10

p10

p9

note the notched primaries of male

p10

p10

p5 similar in length to p6 and p7

p5 shorter than p6 and p7 compared with Tropical

forked tail

forked tail

Tropical

Couch's

due to longer p5, Tropical often has appearance of more rounded wing tip than Couch's

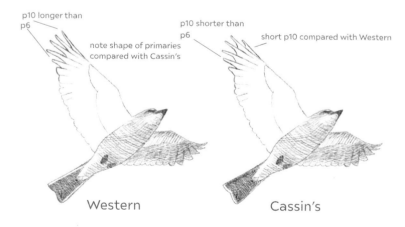

p10 longer than p6

note shape of primaries compared with Cassin's

p10 shorter than p6

short p10 compared with Western

Western

Cassin's

Tropical Kingbird
Tyrannus melancholicus
L 7.2–9.1″ (18.4–23.0 cm), WT 1.13–1.50 oz (32.0–42.5 g)

GENERAL IDENTIFICATION The Tropical Kingbird looks like
a generic yellow kingbird, but there are important distinguishing
features to note. Tropical Kingbird has a short primary projection
(compared with Western and Cassin's), dark brown forked tail,
brown wings, pale edges to greater and median coverts, slightly
greenish back, bright yellow underside, dingy yellow chest, medium-
gray crown, and darkish face, often with contrasting dark auriculars,
which give it a somewhat masked appearance. Juvenal plumage is
like adult, but overall plumage is more contrasting. Adult Tropicals
have concealed red in the crown (lacking in juveniles). Its yellow
belly grades gradually into a dingy upper chest. The color contrast
between the dark brown tail and wings is weak. The pale edges to
the greater and median coverts give a scaly look to the wing and the
impression of dull wingbars. In fresh plumage (winter to spring for
adults, fall for juveniles), Tropical's outer primaries usually have thin,
pale edges on their outer margins. From a distance, the primary wing
panel on the folded wing thus looks lighter instead of solid black,
resulting in weak wing panel contrast (compared with Couch's).
Beware of worn birds (typically late summer for adults), which may
make the wing panel contrast difficult to assess. Note also that the
primary wing panel can be difficult to see during the middle of the
day as it is often in the shade of the secondaries on a folded wing.

Structurally, Tropical has a slender, somewhat elongated build
compared with other yellow-bellied kingbirds, including Couch's.
Tropical's tail often appears long, accentuated by its short primary
projection. Its bill is long and slender. When combined with
its flattish crown, Tropical has a mean look. The short primary
projection (compared with Western and Eastern) is noticeable in
flight as the outer primaries do not protrude much beyond the
projected outline of the inner primaries.

For the advanced birder, attention to wing formula may be useful. The short primary projection of Tropical and Couch's compared with that of Western and Cassin's is also manifested in the primary pattern on the folded and spread wing. In Tropical and Couch's, the outermost primaries (p7 to p10) are short compared with Western and Cassin's, such that on the folded wing, only the tips of p4 to p6 (sometimes p7) are visible (p7 to p10 usually hidden beneath p5 and p6). In Tropical, the gap between the tips of p5 and p6 is distinctly shorter than the gap between the tips of p5 and p4 on the folded wing (see plates on pp. 113, 114, and 130). In Couch's, the same gaps are more similar in width. In other words, p6 projects only slightly beyond p5 in Tropical, a manifestation of Tropical's short primary projection (compared with Couch's). When the tips of p4, p5, and p6 can be seen, the relative difference in primary tip gaps can be useful in separating Couch's from Tropical. Of course, beware when p4 is hidden beneath the secondary stack, which is often the case. Wear and molt can also make it challenging to judge these features, even with good photographs.

In flight, Tropical's outer primaries (p5 to p10) protrude slightly further beyond the inner primaries than in Couch's (but much less so than in Western). On the spread wing of Tropical, p5 is similar in length to p6 and p7 (p5 is short in Couch's), such that the tips of p5, p6, and p7 are more colinear. Specifically, the angle between the line connecting the tips of p6 and p7, and the line connecting p7 and p5, is generally more acute (9–18°) than that in Couch's (15–26°) on a spread wing. These wing formula features are very challenging to see in the field but can be studied with good photographs of spread wings from below. Wing formula field marks should not be applied to birds in molt.

Outer primary feathers in adult males are notched on the inner web, resulting in tapered and pointed outer primaries. Notches are less apparent in females and lacking in juveniles. Tropical's prebasic molt may commence on breeding grounds but is mostly completed (flight feathers) on wintering grounds. In July and Aug., adult birds will have highly worn flight feathers.

VOCALIZATIONS Tropical's calls and songs are best described as rapid and accelerating high-pitched twitters, reminiscent of an insect, like a katydid. Tropical's songs are generally simple, composed only of twitters, without the slurred or burry phrases of other yellow-bellied kingbird vocalizations. Fork-tailed Flycatcher has a similar twitter.

HABITAT, DISTRIBUTION, AND SEASONAL STATUS Tropical prefers semi-open habitats with scattered trees or other tall structures, including buildings. It is found in riparian edges, parks, farmland, and rural areas, often near water, frequently perched on structures including tall snags and fences. Tropical's nest is an open bowl loosely constructed with twigs and grass, usually placed in the crotch of branches in medium to tall trees or in tangled wires or recesses in utility poles. Its nests are often conspicuously exposed.

Tropical Kingbird breeds in southeastern Arizona south along the Pacific slope of western Mexico and from southernmost Texas south along the Caribbean slope of Mexico to the Yucatan Peninsula and Central America (small numbers have begun breeding in west Texas). Its range continues south through northern South America and across the Amazon basin. Four subspecies have been described: *T. m. satrapa* in southern Texas and eastern Mexico south to northern South America; *T. m. occidentalis* in western Mexico and southeastern Arizona; *T. m. despotes* in northeastern Brazil; and *T. m. melancholicus* across most of South America, excluding the regions occupied by *satrapa* and *despotes*. The subspecies *satrapa*, *occidentalis*, and *melancholicus* are migratory. Tropical vacates its breeding grounds in southeastern Arizona and northwestern Mexico by Sept., returning to breed in mid-Apr. Southern Texas birds are generally present year-round although they are much more abundant in the Rio Grande Valley. In the Southern Hemisphere, Tropicals (*melancholicus*) vacate their southern breeding grounds of northern Argentina and Uruguay by mid-Apr. and move north into the Amazonian basin during the southern winter. Southern Hemisphere birds begin to move south during late Aug. and by mid-Oct. have spread across northern Argentina to breed during the southern summer.

Although Tropical's breeding range in the United States is primarily restricted to southeastern Arizona and southern Texas, it is known to wander widely. It is a regular fall vagrant along the Pacific coast from Baja California north to Washington, with occasional records as far north as southeastern Alaska. It is also a regular fall vagrant to the Atlantic coast of the United States but in lower numbers than on the Pacific coast. Most fall vagrants are first-cycle birds. Fall vagrants appear by Sept., peaking in Oct. Many fall vagrants linger into late fall, with a few lingering through the winter, especially on the Pacific coast. Vagrancy also occurs in spring, but much less frequently than in fall. Most spring vagrants are found in eastern North America between May and July. Presumably, most if not all vagrants are of the northern subspecies *satrapa* and *occidentalis*, which are inseparable in the field. However, it may be worth scrutinizing vagrants, especially during the northern spring, for the southern migratory subspecies *melancholicus*, which has a slightly darker crown and face, and a greener chest; but more work is necessary to sort out subspecies identification.

SIMILAR SPECIES Tropical Kingbird has a much shorter primary projection than Western and Cassin's. A lack of white outer margins to tail should rule out Western, but in bad lighting or in worn birds it may be difficult to rely on the absence of white in the tail to identify a potential Tropical or Couch's. Tropical's tail is usually forked, whereas the tails of Western and Cassin's are usually square tipped (although beware of juvenile Western and Cassin's, which can have slightly forked tails). Tropical's tail is dark but usually not as dark as in Western and Cassin's. Tropical's chest is dingy yellow, grading gradually into its bright yellow underparts. Western and Cassin's have gray chests, which contrast with their yellow bellies. Tropical's bill tends to be longer than the bills of Western and Cassin's. Tropical's high-pitched twitter is diagnostic enough to rule out Western and Cassin's.

Distinguishing Tropical from Couch's is more challenging. Vocalizations are the most reliable field mark as Tropical's songs and calls are long, high-pitched twitters, akin to a Vermilion Flycatcher (*Pyrocephalus rubinus*). The calls of Couch's Kingbird consist of long, drawn-out burry slurs and single, clipped "*pip*" calls. When vocalizations are not heard, structure and color contrast may help. Overall, Tropical has a slenderer body and a narrower bill compared with Couch's. Although there is overlap, Tropical tends to have a shorter primary projection than Couch's, giving the impression that Tropical has a slightly longer tail. Tropical's tail is often more deeply forked than Couch's and rarely squared off. Tropical also tends to have a flatter crown compared with Couch's more rounded crown. Its flatter crown and straighter bill give Tropical a meaner look than Couch's. Although both have yellow underparts, Tropical's chest tends to be dingy yellow whereas Couch's chest is usually bright yellow. The bright yellow chest of Couch's contrasts with its gray head and white throat. This contrast between chest and throat is diminished in Tropical because Tropical's throat is grayer. Often, the underparts of Couch's are brighter yellow than Tropical. Tropical's auriculars tend to be darker and more extensive than in Couch's.

Good images of spread wings may be useful in separating Tropical from Couch's as the lengths of outer primaries differ in these two species (see discussion in General Identification). In Tropical, p5 is similar in length to p6 and p7, such that the tips of p5 to p7 are more colinear than in Couch's on a spread wing. Note also the relative differences in primary tip spacings between p4 and p5, and between p5 and p6 on a folded wing. On Tropical's folded wing, p6 projects only slightly beyond p5, whereas in Couch's, p6 projects further beyond p5.

Another important distinguishing feature, when seen well, is the nature of the secondary and primary wing panel contrast. In Tropical, the primaries tend to have pale edges, but in Couch's, the edges of primaries are darker (avoid using this field mark to identify worn birds in the summer). Tropical's wings are also slightly blacker than those of Couch's. In particular, the secondaries of Couch's have dark brown ground color and pale edges, creating greater contrast with the blackish ground color of the primaries. In Tropical, the secondaries and primaries are both black or both dark brown. Collectively, the secondary and primary feather patterns and colors give Tropical a weaker wing panel contrast than Couch's. Wing panel contrast should, of course, be used with care when examining worn birds or in poor lighting.

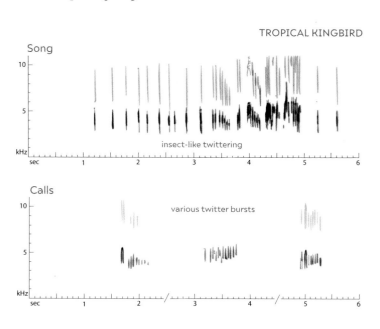

TROPICAL KINGBIRD

TROPICAL KINGBIRD

often shows charcoal gray auriculars

long bill

greenish back

short primary projection

weak wing panel contrast

often pale edges to primaries

dingy chest

bright yellow

more rounded wing tip

Tropical

Western

bright yellow underparts

Tropical Kingbird

Western Kingbird

usually deeply forked tail

TROPICAL KINGBIRD

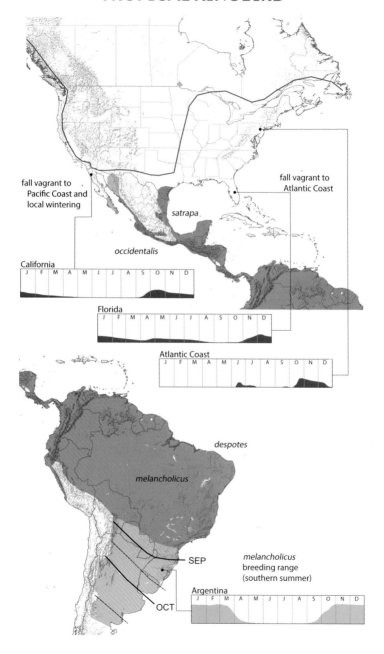

fall vagrant to
Pacific Coast and
local wintering

satrapa

fall vagrant to
Atlantic Coast

occidentalis

California

J	F	M	A	M	J	J	A	S	O	N	D

Florida

J	F	M	A	M	J	J	A	S	O	N	D

Atlantic Coast

J	F	M	A	M	J	J	A	S	O	N	D

despotes

melancholicus

SEP

melancholicus
breeding range
(southern summer)

OCT

Argentina

J	F	M	A	M	J	J	A	S	O	N	D

Couch's Kingbird

Tyrannus couchii

L 7.9–9.4″ (20.1–23.9 cm), WT 1.37–1.41 oz (38.9–40.0 g)

GENERAL IDENTIFICATION This yellow-bellied kingbird from southern Texas is a much sought-after vagrant in other parts of the United States. When studying a possible Couch's Kingbird, focus first on vocalizations as its calls are unique. Key plumage characteristics include bright yellow underparts and chest, dark brown tail (not as black as in Western), brown wings (secondaries and covert feathers), greenish mantle, pale edges to greater and median coverts, and gray head and face. Adults have concealed red in the crown (lacking in juveniles). Juvenal plumage is overall like adult, but with slightly buffier tips to wing coverts and more contrasting facial pattern. Couch's gray head often has a subtle tint of blue, appearing slightly colder in color than Tropical's gray. Like Tropical, Couch's often shows a darkish ear patch, but the ear patch is generally less contrasting and less extensive than Tropical's. Couch's does not display significant color contrast between its chest and belly because both are typically bright yellow. However, the generally bright yellow chest contrasts with the white throat and gray head. Pale edges to greater and median coverts give the impression of dull wingbars. In fresh plumage (late fall and winter), Couch's primaries generally lack pale edges, making the primary wing panel appear solid black, contrasting with the brownish secondaries. The secondary wing panel has a browner ground color and bright, pale feather edges. These features give Couch's a relatively strong wing panel contrast (but beware of worn birds).

Structurally, Couch's has a bulging chest, and its crown is often rounded. Its bill is medium in length with a convex culmen, giving a slightly conical impression to the bill shape. Couch's tail ranges from shallowly forked to squarish. Because its primary projection is shorter than in Western and Cassin's, its outer primaries do not protrude as much beyond the outline of the inner primaries and secondaries as in Western and Cassin's.

For the advanced birder, the detailed wing formula can be used to separate Couch's Kingbird from Tropical. In Couch's, p5 is shorter than p6 and p7 (similar length in Tropical). Thus, on a spread wing, the tips of p5, p6, and p7 are less colinear, with p6 noticeably protruding beyond a line connecting the tips of p5 and p7 (see discussion under Tropical Kingbird). The angle between the p5 to p7 and p6 to p7 lines in Couch's is generally less acute than that in Tropical. These differences in the lengths of outer primaries are also visible on the folded wing in good photographs. As for Tropical, p7 to p10 in Couch's are generally hidden on the folded wing. However, in Couch's, p6 projects further beyond p5 than in Tropical, a manifestation of Couch's slightly longer primary projection. This projection can be quantified by comparing the relative widths of the p5 to p6 gap and the p5 to p4 gap if all three primary tips are visible (p4 is often hidden beneath secondaries on folded wing).

The shapes of outer primaries are useful in aging and sexing. Outer primaries of adult male Couch's are distinctly notched, manifested as tapered outer primary tips. Notching is reduced in females and absent in juvenal plumage. Prebasic molt begins on breeding grounds but completes on wintering grounds.

VOCALIZATIONS Couch's emits a distinctive high-pitched, burry "*BReeer*," characterized by an initial rise in pitch followed by a long, drawn-out descending coda. These calls can be given singly or in short continuous succession. Couch's also gives short, isolated "*pip*" calls, frequently in association with its longer burry call. Occasionally, it gives a short squeaky "*eek*" call. Song consists of a series of 2–5 short "*puwi*" phrases preceding a rapid train of high-pitched *pips*, short twitters, or descending slurs (e.g., "*puwi-puwi-puwi-eo*").

HABITAT, DISTRIBUTION, AND SEASONAL STATUS Like Tropical, Couch's Kingbird prefers semi-open habitats with scattered tall trees and structures, and is often found near water. Where their ranges overlap, Couch's frequents a broader variety of habitats, including slightly more brushy habitats, whereas Tropical is often found closer to water or around buildings. Couch's nest is an open bowl loosely constructed of twigs and various plant fibers. The nest is attached to thin branches within the outer canopy of medium to tall trees, and occasionally in tall utility poles.

Couch's Kingbird is primarily a year-round resident throughout southern Texas and south along the Caribbean slope of Mexico to the Yucatan Peninsula. However, it undergoes local seasonal movements. In winter, southern Texas birds seem to move south into Mexico and north to the northern Gulf of Mexico. Between mid-Mar. and early Apr. numbers build up again in southern Texas, presumably due to individuals returning from the south and north to breed. In the United States, Couch's Kingbird is very rare away from Texas and the Texas-Louisiana coast. Vagrants have been recorded as far west as Arizona and California, north to Michigan, and east to New England, Maryland, and Florida. Vagrancy beyond Texas and Louisiana is restricted to the fall (Nov. to Dec.), with some, particularly in the west, lingering through the end of Jan. Couch's vagrancy is far outnumbered by Tropical, but it is possible that vagrant Couch's have been overlooked.

SIMILAR SPECIES Separation from Western and Cassin's Kingbirds is usually straightforward, although a surprising number of Western Kingbirds are misidentified as Couch's in Texas. Visiting birders to Texas are often intent on finding a Couch's, and often assume a yellow-bellied kingbird with a "*pip*" call is a Couch's; however, Western gives a very similar call. Before exploring Couch's and

Tropical, be sure to rule out Western (or Cassin's) first. Western has white outer margins to the tail and Cassin's often has pale tips to the tail. Western and Cassin's also have very long primary projections. Couch's chest is yellow whereas Western and Cassin's chests are gray. Couch's tail can be shallowly forked at times, but Western and Cassin's are less often forked. Cassin's and Western have blacker tails than Couch's and Tropical.

Separation from Tropical Kingbird is straightforward if vocalizations are heard (Tropical gives a high-pitched twittering call), but silent birds can be challenging and sometimes best left unidentified. Focusing on a combination of structure and plumage contrasts is essential. Couch's chest tends to be brighter yellow than the dingy yellow chest of Tropical. Compared with Tropical, Couch's bright yellow chest tends to contrast more with the gray upperparts and white throat. Tropical's throat is light gray and blends into its dingy chest and gray face. Couch's auriculars are usually not as dark as in Tropical. Structurally, Couch's crown is round and Tropical's flatter, and its bill tends to be shorter, thicker, and more convex along the culmen than Tropical's more slender, longer, and straighter bill. Its chest tends to bulge out more than Tropical's. Couch's primary projection is subtly longer than that of Tropical (although there is overlap). If wing formula can be studied, pay attention to the relative lengths of the outer primaries (see Tropical Kingbird for additional details). On a folded wing, p6 projects farther beyond p5 than in Tropical (pp. 113, 114, and 130). Finally, in fresh plumage (fall to winter), Couch's has a stronger wing panel contrast than Tropical. In Couch's, the primary wing panel is usually black with limited pale edges to the primaries, but in Tropical, pale edges to primaries make Tropical's primary panel look lighter.

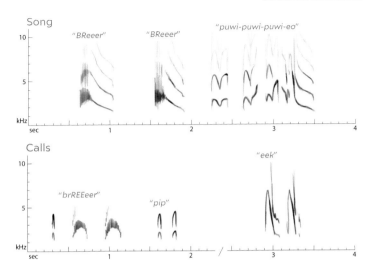

COUCH'S KINGBIRD

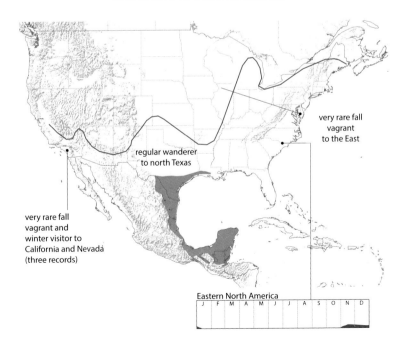

COUCH'S KINGBIRD

slightly shorter, more conical bill

short primary projection, but longer than Tropical

chest brighter yellow than Tropical

strong contrast between yellow chest and white throat

dark primary wing panel

outer primary (p10) shorter than others

more pointed wing with long outer 4 primaries (p7–p10) of similar length

tail often less forked than Tropical

Couch's

Western

TROPICAL AND COUCH'S

longer bill

shorter, conical bill

Tropical

Couch's

brighter chest and whiter throat

primary projection slightly longer than Tropical

Tropical

more extensive green wash across chest

stronger contrast with whiter throat and bright chest

Couch's

tail often more deeply forked

tail often less forked

TROPICAL AND COUCH'S

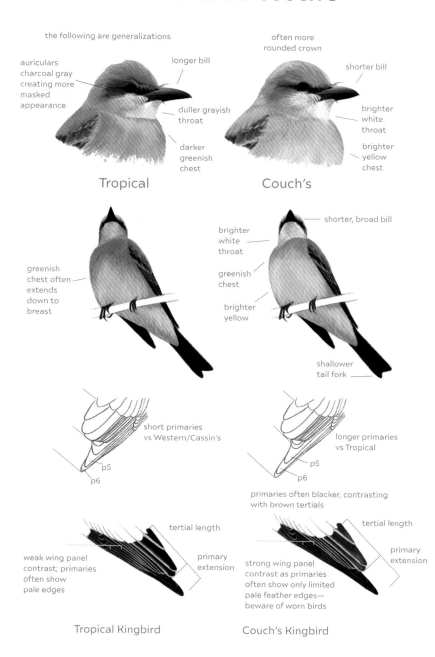

the following are generalizations

auriculars charcoal gray creating more masked appearance

longer bill

duller grayish throat

darker greenish chest

Tropical

often more rounded crown

shorter bill

brighter white throat

brighter yellow chest

Couch's

greenish chest often extends down to breast

brighter white throat

greenish chest

brighter yellow

shorter, broad bill

shallower tail fork

short primaries vs Western/Cassin's

p5

p6

longer primaries vs Tropical

p5

p6

primaries often blacker, contrasting with brown tertials

weak wing panel contrast; primaries often show pale edges

tertial length

primary extension

strong wing panel contrast as primaries often show only limited pale feather edges— beware of worn birds

tertial length

primary extension

Tropical Kingbird

Couch's Kingbird

Cassin's Kingbird

Tyrannus vociferans

L 8.3–9.2″ (21.1–23.4 cm), WT 1.41–1.61 oz (40.2–45.6 g)

GENERAL IDENTIFICATION Cassin's Kingbird is a common bird in open forests or riparian edges in western North America. It is often found perched high on dead branches in tall trees, from which it frequently vocalizes. Cassin's has a dark gray head, face, mantle, and chest, which contrast strongly with its white chin and lower cheek, and bright yellow underparts. Cassin's has concealed red in its crown (lacking in juveniles). Its lores and auriculars tend to be dark, almost black, giving it a masked appearance and enhancing the contrast between the dark gray head and white chin. In particular, the white cheek does not extend past the eye and imparts a distinctive and diagnostic face pattern. Cassin's often shows a thin gray malar stripe, unique to the kingbirds (although the malar stripe is not always present).

Cassin's tail is dark brown. On fresh birds, the tail often shows pale tips. This feature is unique among the yellow-bellied kingbirds, but often the pale tips are difficult to see or worn out. Cassin's tail generally lacks the bright white outer margin of Western Kingbird, but it occasionally shows a pale gray outer margin that could be confused with Western. Its dark tail contrasts with its brown wings. Pale edges of median and greater covert feathers give Cassin's brighter wingbars than most other yellow-bellied kingbirds. Juvenal plumage is like adult, but upperparts may be slightly brownish.

Like Western Kingbird, outer primary feathers are long, resulting in a very long primary projection on the folded wing. Unlike Tropical and Couch's, all the outer primaries (except for p10) are visible on the folded wing. In flight, long outer primaries noticeably project beyond the inner primaries, unlike the more rounded outer primaries of Tropical and Couch's; p10 of Cassin's is distinctly shorter than p9 (similar length in Western), although this can only be seen on a spread wing. Primary tip spacing on the folded wing of

Cassin's is uneven due to the presence of a wide gap between p5 and p4 in the exposed primaries on a folded wing (more even spacing in Western). Outer primaries are notched in males, resulting in tapered or attenuated primary tips (usually only visible in spread wings). Notching is less apparent in females and lacking in juveniles. The prebasic molt is completed on breeding grounds, migratory stopovers, or on wintering grounds.

VOCALIZATIONS The most frequently given call of Cassin's Kingbird is a loud and distinctive "*chi-keeer*," which can be heard from afar (reminiscent of Ash-throated Flycatcher's "*chi-keeer*" call from a distance). Other frequent calls include burry "*brEER*" and "*breEEer*" calls (slightly lower frequency and shorter in length than those of Couch's) and various low-pitched chatters. Cassin's occasionally gives a descending "*chew*" call. Its song, commonly given pre-dawn, consists of an undulating series of burry "*breEEer*" notes and short descending "*kew*" notes ("*br-br-KEW*" or "*bar-be-CUE*"), often accelerating in tempo and increasing in volume (e.g., crescendo) at the end of the song ("*bar-be-CUE——WHATCHA-GONna-do*"). The song is unlike that of most other kingbirds but includes some phrases reminiscent of Brown-crested Flycatcher and Great Kiskadee (*Pitangus sulphuratus*).

HABITAT, DISTRIBUTION, AND SEASONAL STATUS Cassin's Kingbird prefers semi-open areas, from fields with scattered trees to open woodlands and shrublands. It can be found in a variety of ecological zones, including chaparral, riparian edges, oak savanna, pinyon-juniper forests, open pine forests, and eucalyptus groves. Its preferred habitat overlaps slightly with that of Western Kingbird, but it prefers habitats with a higher density of vegetation. Cassin's can be found from lowland areas into foothills. Nests are open bowls constructed of twigs and various plant fibers mixed with dry leaves built beneath the canopy of tall trees.

Cassin's is a common year-round resident in open oak woodlands of coastal California from the central coast through southern California and the Pacific slope of northern Baja California. In Mexico, it is a widespread year-round resident in the foothills of Sonora and central Mexico south to Nicaragua. It is largely absent from the low elevation deserts of the lower Colorado River in southeastern California and southwestern Arizona because of the lack of appropriate habitat. In mid-Mar. birds from Mexico expand north into interior western United States to breed. Its breeding range includes the foothills of southeastern Arizona to western Texas, the Colorado Plateau, and the foothills of the eastern Rocky Mountains. Migrants regularly pass through central Texas. Southward movements in fall begin in July, with wintering birds in Baja California Sur appearing in mid-July. By mid-Oct. to early Nov. most individuals in the interior western United States have vacated the region, although small numbers regularly winter in southeastern Arizona. It is a rare but regular fall migrant and winter visitor to Louisiana and Florida, and possibly elsewhere along the Gulf of Mexico. In the northeastern United States and the Midwest, it is a very rare vagrant, with most being recorded in late fall. Spring vagrants to eastern North America are exceptionally scarce and mostly confined to the Midwest between mid-May and early June (these possibly pertain to spring migration overshoots).

SIMILAR SPECIES Cassin's Kingbird is commonly confused with Western Kingbird because of range overlap. When tail color patterns are seen, identification is straightforward. However, beware of backlighting, which can give the impression of white outer margins to the tail in Cassin's, and feather wear, which can erode the white outer margins of Western tails and white tail tips of Cassin's. Note that some Cassin's may show pale outer-tail margin, but never immaculate white as in Western. When the tail cannot be seen well, focus on relative plumage contrasts. Cassin's is a darker and more contrasty bird than Western. Its white chin does not extend past the eye. Its chest is dark gray, whereas Western has a paler gray chest. Western's lores and auriculars are usually light gray, not blackish as in Cassin's. Cassin's wingbars are more evident than Western's. Unlike Western, primary tip spacing is uneven, with a large gap between the outer primaries. Both species have dark tails, contrasting with the wings, but Western's tail, being jet black, is darker than the tail of Cassin's, which has a slight brownish cast. Cassin's calls and songs consist of short burry phrases unlike the twitters, chatters, and squeaky notes of Western.

Cassin's dark face and bright yellow underparts impart some resemblance to Tropical and Couch's Kingbirds. However, Cassin's has a distinctly longer primary projection than Tropical and Couch's. Cassin's wings are brown, contrasting with its black tail. Cassin's chest is dark gray, whereas Tropical and Couch's have yellower chests (especially Couch's). Tropical's tail is often distinctly forked, unlike the squared off tail of Cassin's. The darker and slightly grayer mantle of Cassin's differs from the light olive-gray mantles of Tropical and Couch's. The burry calls of Cassin's are distinct from the high-pitched twitters of Tropical but can be superficially like the calls of Couch's, which are best described as burry slurs, "*brEEer*," whereas the calls of Cassin's tend to include more discrete notes, "*chi-keer*."

CASSIN'S KINGBIRD

adult patch of red crown feathers rarely ever seen

black mask

dark mantle

white cheek does not extend past eye

white chin

long primary projection

gray chest

long primaries compared with Tropical

pale edges to coverts

pale tips to generally square-ended tail

Undertails

beware some birds can show pale outer web to outer-tail

long primary projection compared with Tropical/ Couch's

Western   Cassin's   Note blacker underside of tail on Western

Song

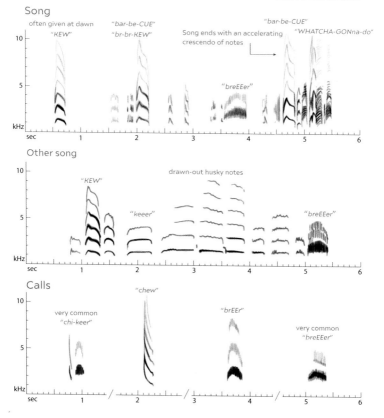

often given at dawn

"KEW"

"bar-be-CUE"
"br-br-KEW"

"bar-be-CUE"

Song ends with an accelerating
crescendo of notes

"WHATCHA-GONna-do"

"breEEer"

Other song

drawn-out husky notes

"KEW"

"keeer"

"breEEer"

Calls

"chew"

very common
"chi-keer"

"brEEr"

very common
"breEEer"

CASSIN'S KINGBIRD

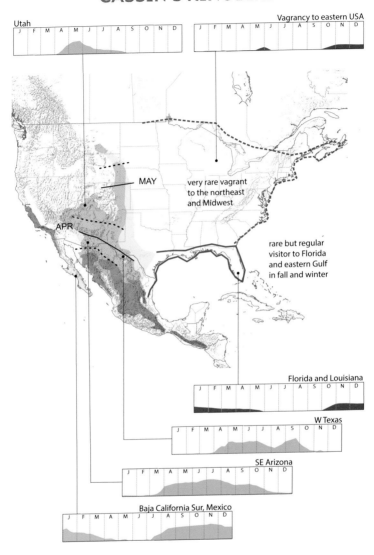

Utah

J	F	M	A	M	J	J	A	S	O	N	D

Vagrancy to eastern USA

J	F	M	A	M	J	J	A	S	O	N	D

MAY

APR

very rare vagrant
to the northeast
and Midwest

rare but regular
visitor to Florida
and eastern Gulf
in fall and winter

Florida and Louisiana

J	F	M	A	M	J	J	A	S	O	N	D

W Texas

J	F	M	A	M	J	J	A	S	O	N	D

SE Arizona

J	F	M	A	M	J	J	A	S	O	N	D

Baja California Sur, Mexico

J	F	M	A	M	J	J	A	S	O	N	D

Western Kingbird

Tyrannus verticalis

L 8.0–9.5″ (20.3–24.1 cm), WT 1.3–1.8 oz (36.9–51.0 g)

GENERAL IDENTIFICATION The Western Kingbird is one of the most iconic birds of open areas and grasslands in western North America. It often perches conspicuously on telephone wires, fence posts, or tall isolated trees. It is a very vocal bird, frequently twittering from its perch or as it hovers and flutters in the air. Highly territorial, it can often be seen chasing and harassing potential predators, such as hawks. Western Kingbird has a light gray head and chest, yellowish belly, dark brown wings, and a jet black tail that contrasts with browner wings. The tail has conspicuous white outer-tail margins (outer web of outermost tail is immaculate white), which are unique to this species (although Cassin's can show pale gray outer margins). The chin is whitish and extends past the eye unlike Cassin's. Also, unlike Cassin's, the white chin grades into the gray face, showing much less contrast with the gray head and chest. Western's mantle is light gray with a dull olive or greenish wash. Its gray chest and upperparts show medium contrast with its yellow belly. Western has concealed red or orange in its crown (lacking in juveniles).

Western has the longest primary projection of the yellow-bellied kingbirds, accentuated in the male by pointy and highly tapered outer primary tips; female's primary tips are less attenuated. The outermost primary, p10, is long and of similar length to p9 (p10 is short in Cassin's). Western's primary tips are equally spaced on a folded wing. In flight, the long outermost primaries tend to project outward beyond the inner primaries. The tail tip is usually square (occasionally forked in juveniles). The greater and median coverts typically do not show pale feather edges except in worn late summer birds, when feathers are frayed. In these worn birds, the white margins of the outer-tail feather may be dull or even completely eroded. The yellow on the underparts can vary from bright to pale lemon yellow, especially on worn summer birds. The prebasic molt begins on breeding grounds or migratory stopovers but completes (flight feathers) on wintering grounds, so most birds in late summer/ early fall in the United States are in worn plumage (first-year birds may appear fresher).

VOCALIZATIONS Western's songs and calls are best described as various combinations of rapid twitters, chatters, and squeaky phrases. Twitters are composed of short, staccato *"pip"* notes, emitted in rapid succession. Chatters are composed of short, rapidly repeated notes (*"ch-ch-ch-ch-ch-ch"*), somewhat reminiscent of blackbird and cowbird rattles or even oriole chatters. Squeaky phrases often have a higher pitch than twitters and chatters. Its dawn song consists of chatters interspersed with squeaky phrases. Its flight songs usually consist of a mix of twitters and chatters. Its common agitated call is composed mostly of twitters. Western often gives single note *"pip"* calls from its perch.

HABITAT, DISTRIBUTION, AND SEASONAL STATUS Western Kingbirds prefer open areas scattered with tall trees or other tall structures. They are often found perched on telephone lines or barbed wire fences along rural roads. If these microhabitat conditions are met, they can be found in a wide variety of ecological zones, including grasslands, desert scrub, dry and open forests, and urban and suburban settings. They commonly frequent the edges of riparian woodlands in arid environments. Western's habitat preference may overlap with that of Cassin's, but Western tends to prefer more open habitats. Its nest is an open bowl constructed of twigs and various plant fibers, typically placed on a branch within the canopy of a tall tree or in protected parts of tall utility poles.

Western Kingbird spends its summers in lowland areas of the western United States and winters in central Mexico south through Costa Rica. Its breeding range extends from northern Mexico to the Great Plains of southern Canada and east to the Mississippi River. West of the Rocky Mountains, its summer range extends from California, Nevada, and Arizona north into the interior valleys of the Pacific Northwest and southern British Columbia. Breeding birds arrive in coastal California by the second week of Mar. and in southern Texas by early Apr. Birds in the northernmost part of the breeding range arrive in early to mid-May. Birds begin heading back south in July, with most birds departing the United States by early Sept. Wintering birds in Mexico arrive by late Aug. to early Sept.

Western Kingbird wanders widely from its normal range, and during spring migration birds regularly overshoot into the Midwest and east toward the Great Lakes region. Spring vagrants have been documented as far north as Alaska. It is an uncommon but regular fall vagrant along the Atlantic coast, with some birds lingering into the winter. It is an uncommon winter visitor to the Gulf of Mexico coast and especially Florida, where small wintering groups can be found locally.

SIMILAR SPECIES Western Kingbird is structurally like Cassin's with its long primary projection, but it is overall a paler and less contrasty bird than Cassin's. In Cassin's, the darker gray head contrasts more strongly with the white chin than in Western. The white chin of Cassin's does not extend past the eye, as in Western. Compared with Western, the darker chest of Cassin's contrasts more strongly with its yellow underparts. When seen well, the presence of white outer margins to the tail are usually diagnostic for Western, whereas white edges to the tail tip are diagnostic for Cassin's. However, beware of worn Westerns, in which the white margin of the tail can become severely reduced. Conversely, frayed tail feathers in worn Cassin's can often give the impression of white (instead of pale) outer margins to the tail, especially when backlit. Cassin's has noticeable wingbars, while Western generally lacks wingbars. Cassin's mantle tends to be darker gray than the paler greenish-gray mantle of Western. Western's underparts range from bright yellow to pale yellow, while the underparts of Cassin's are usually bright yellow. Exposed primary tips on the folded wing of Western tend to be evenly spaced, unlike the more uneven spacing of those of Cassin's. Although both species have dark tails compared with their wings, Western's tail is noticeably blacker than that of Cassin's. The calls and songs of Cassin's do not contain the staccato twitter and chatter phrases of Western. In terms of habitat, Western prefers more open areas than Cassin's.

Western can be easily confused with Tropical and Couch's Kingbirds, but white outer margins to the tail are diagnostic of Western when seen. However, the most reliable distinguishing mark, apart from vocalizations, is Western's much longer primary projection compared with Tropical and Couch's. These differences can even be seen in flying birds, with Westerns showing longer outer wings than Tropical and Couch's. Western has a grayish chest, whereas the chests of Tropical and Couch's are more yellowish. The tail is square tipped in Western but often forked in Tropical and Couch's. Western's tail is also blacker than in Tropical and Couch's. Tropical and Couch's have pale edges to greater and median coverts, resulting in more conspicuous wingbars compared with Western. Western's vocalizations are unlikely to be confused with Couch's, which does not twitter. Western's twitter calls superficially resemble that of Tropical, but Tropical's calls and songs usually consist only of twitters (higher pitched than Western's) whereas Western's vocalizations will usually include chatters or squeaky phrases.

WESTERN KINGBIRD

uniformly patterned wings without contrasting pale edges to coverts

light gray chest

long primary projection

juvenile can show pale edges to coverts like Cassin's

pinkish base to bill

compare bill and head shape with Cassin's

white outer web to outer tail feather

can show notched tail

long primary projection compared with Tropical/Couch's

WESTERN KINGBIRD

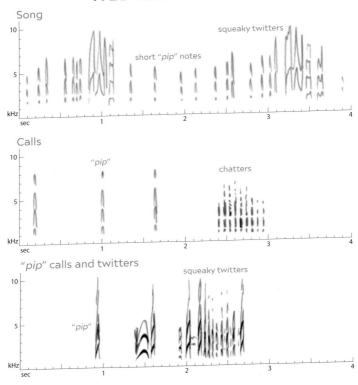

Song

squeaky twitters

short *"pip"* notes

Calls

"pip"

chatters

"pip" calls and twitters

squeaky twitters

"pip"

WESTERN KINGBIRD

Spring Migration

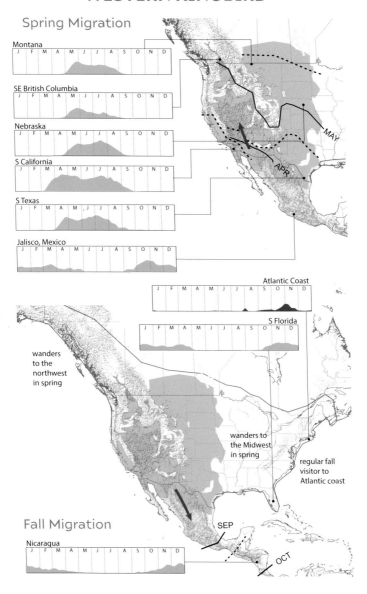

Montana
| J | F | M | A | M | J | J | A | S | O | N | D |

SE British Columbia
| J | F | M | A | M | J | J | A | S | O | N | D |

Nebraska
| J | F | M | A | M | J | J | A | S | O | N | D |

S California
| J | F | M | A | M | J | J | A | S | O | N | D |

S Texas
| J | F | M | A | M | J | J | A | S | O | N | D |

Jalisco, Mexico
| J | F | M | A | M | J | J | A | S | O | N | D |

MAY
APR

Atlantic Coast
| J | F | M | A | M | J | J | A | S | O | N | D |

S Florida
| J | F | M | A | M | J | J | A | S | O | N | D |

wanders to the northwest in spring

wanders to the Midwest in spring

regular fall visitor to Atlantic coast

Fall Migration

Nicaragua
| J | F | M | A | M | J | J | A | S | O | N | D |

SEP
OCT

WESTERN AND CASSIN'S KINGBIRDS

Western

note differences in head pattern

bold white outer tail

gray on face below eye

Cassin's

white chin

paler edges to coverts

shorter-tailed than Western

light gray chest

darker chest

narrower outer primaries on male Western vs male Cassin's

Western

Cassin's

shorter outer primary

bold white outer tail, but care needed as Cassin's can show pale fringes to outer tail

more evenly spaced primaries

large step in spacing

Western

Cassin's

Western

Cassin's

Western

Cassin's

Western

Cassin's

note jet black undertail on Western vs duller tail on Cassin's

Thick-billed Kingbird

Tyrannus crassirostris

L 8.7–9.4″ (22.1–23.9 cm), WT 1.8–2.1 oz (51.0–59.5 g)

GENERAL IDENTIFICATION The Thick-billed Kingbird is nearly unmistakable because of its large and bulk body, and very thick bill. It is a bird of riparian woodlands, where it prefers to sit on the tops of trees and large bushes, often on exposed branches. It has dark gray-brown upperparts, a contrasting white throat, and a whitish to pale yellow belly (juvenal birds are more yellow). It has concealed yellow in its crown (lacking in juveniles). This stocky bird has a proportionately larger head and thicker neck compared with other kingbirds. Its tail is shorter and wider, and the tail tip ranges from slightly forked to square. Its primary projection is short compared with Cassin's and Western Kingbirds. In flight, Thick-billed gives the impression of a heavy bird with short wings. The prebasic molt begins on summering grounds between July and Sept. but completes on wintering grounds.

VOCALIZATIONS Thick-billed's song, often given at dawn, consists of a low-pitched twitter followed by a squeaky coda. It gives a variety of short squeaky calls, including a high-pitched and rising "*chuEE*" or "*k-chuEE*" and a high-pitched drawn-out "*chi-KEEeer*," the latter higher in pitch than the similar call of Couch's. Thick-billed also gives a call series consisting of variable squeaky chatters, somewhat reminiscent of Western Kingbird.

HABITAT, DISTRIBUTION, AND SEASONAL STATUS Thick-billed Kingbird prefers riparian woodlands, oak scrub, and thorn forest in desert environments of southeastern United States and western Mexico. In the United States, it is fond of riparian areas with tall cottonwoods and sycamores, where it often perches on dead snags protruding from the crowns of tall trees. When nesting, it often associates with sycamores.

Thick-billed is resident in western Mexico from southern Sonora to Oaxaca. Its range expands north into southeastern Arizona for the nesting season. Birds are on territory in southeastern Arizona by mid-Apr. By mid-Sept., most Arizona birds have departed south. Thick-billed Kingbird is a rare but regular vagrant to southern California, with most records associated with late fall (Oct. to Nov.) vagrants that stay through the winter. These vagrants are often found in eucalyptus groves. Individuals may return to the same tree for several consecutive years. Elsewhere in the United States, it is exceedingly rare as a vagrant (records exist for Colorado, Nevada, North Dakota, Ontario, Texas, and Utah).

SIMILAR SPECIES Thick-billed is unlikely to be confused with any other kingbird due to its large size, large bill, and distinct color pattern. Distant, silhouetted birds, perched high on dead snags, may pose problems, but the stocky body, thick bill, thick neck, and relatively short tail should help distinguish it from other kingbirds.

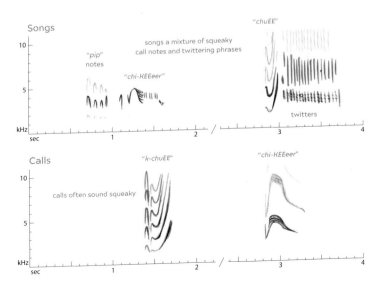

THICK-BILLED KINGBIRD

THICK-BILLED KINGBIRD

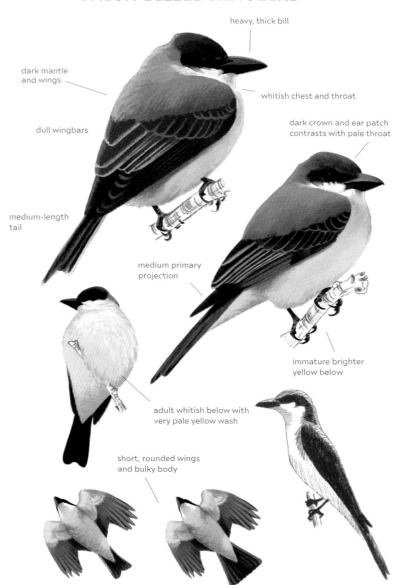

heavy, thick bill

dark mantle and wings

whitish chest and throat

dull wingbars

dark crown and ear patch contrasts with pale throat

medium-length tail

medium primary projection

immature brighter yellow below

adult whitish below with very pale yellow wash

short, rounded wings and bulky body

tail forked from below in flight, but appears square when spread

THICK-BILLED KINGBIRD

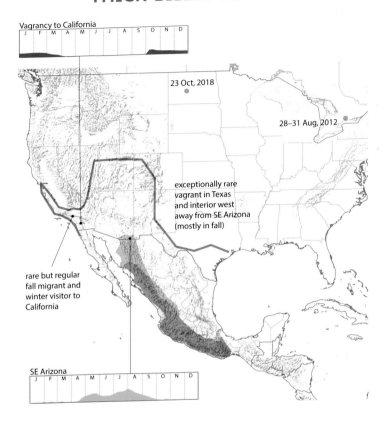

Vagrancy to California

J F M A M J J A S O N D

23 Oct, 2018

28–31 Aug, 2012

exceptionally rare
vagrant in Texas
and interior west
away from SE Arizona
(mostly in fall)

rare but regular
fall migrant and
winter visitor to
California

SE Arizona

J F M A M J J A S O N D

The "white-bellied" kingbirds

Eastern Kingbird

Tyrannus tyrannus

L 7.7–9.1″ (19.5–23.0 cm), WT 1.2–1.8 oz (31.1–51.0 g)

GENERAL IDENTIFICATION The Eastern Kingbird is the only common and widespread kingbird in eastern North America. In the breeding season, it performs aerial courtship displays, hovering and twittering high above the canopy. It is an aggressive bird, chasing potential predators or fighting other kingbirds in the air. With its black-and-white plumage, it is usually unmistakable. Key features are its pale gray chest, white underparts, dark gray mantle, and black face, crown, wings, and tail. The secondaries have bold white edges, and the tail is tipped with white, as if it has been dipped into white paint. Eastern has concealed red or orange in its crown (lacking in juveniles). Eastern has a very long primary projection, presumably because it migrates long distances to its wintering grounds in South America. The bill is medium sized. The prebasic molt occurs almost exclusively on wintering grounds, as is often the case for long-distance migrants.

VOCALIZATIONS Eastern Kingbird's songs and calls are among the highest in pitch of all the kingbirds. It frequently gives a high-pitched, insect-like buzzy call note "*bzzew*" or "*kyer*," typically with a descending quality. It gives a rapid, high-pitched twitter like Tropical and Gray Kingbirds. Calls and songs incorporate various combinations of buzzy notes and twitters.

HABITAT, DISTRIBUTION, AND SEASONAL STATUS Eastern Kingbirds prefer open areas, such as grasslands and agricultural fields, with scattered trees and shrubs. They can often be found along riparian edges near open fields. Eastern Kingbirds commonly perch on top of tall dead snags, powerlines, or fence lines, and are common along rural roads. Nests are open bowls robustly constructed with twigs, grasses, and other plant fibers. The nest is usually placed in the canopy of medium-height trees or shrubs, often somewhat exposed, and occasionally in utility structures. In the western Great Plains, where the ranges of Eastern and Western Kingbirds overlap, the two species can often be found in the same habitat.

Eastern Kingbird is a long-distance migrant, spending summers in eastern North America and wintering in South America, along the eastern slope of the Andes and the western Amazon. Its breeding range extends from eastern Texas to Florida, and north to New England and the prairies of Alberta and eastern British Columbia. It also breeds in intermontane valleys of the central Rocky Mountains and the interior Pacific Northwest. Northbound birds are on the move by mid-Mar. in southern Mexico, arriving in Texas and Florida by late Mar. Birds breeding in the northern part of the breeding range arrive late Apr. to early May. Spring migrants migrate around and across the Gulf of Mexico, often in large flocks. Most birds depart northern breeding grounds by mid-Aug. By late Aug., fall migrants are already passing through Central America, arriving on South American wintering grounds by mid-Sept. Massive flocks winter in the western Amazon. Eastern Kingbird is virtually absent during winter in the United States except for very rare fall stragglers, which may stay into Dec. Of all the kingbirds, Eastern is most prone to wander, presumably because it is a long-distance migrant. It is an uncommon but regular fall and spring vagrant to the Pacific coast, with records as far north as the Arctic Circle in Alaska and Canada. It has also been known to wander across the Atlantic to the western Palearctic and as far south as Patagonia and the Falkland Islands in the South Atlantic Ocean.

SIMILAR SPECIES Eastern Kingbird is usually unmistakable, but in bad lighting it can be confused with Gray. However, Gray is much paler, has darker auriculars, and lacks white tail tips. Gray's bill and tail are distinctly longer than Eastern's, giving it a meaner, bulkier appearance, like Tropical. Loggerhead Kingbird's plumage is like that of Eastern, but Loggerhead is larger in size and has a larger, heavier bill. Female or molting Fork-tailed Flycatchers with slightly shorter tails can look superficially like Eastern because of their similar black-and-white plumage, but Fork-tailed has a lighter mantle and white underwing (Eastern's underwing is dark). Fork-tailed lacks pale edges to secondaries and wing covert feathers.

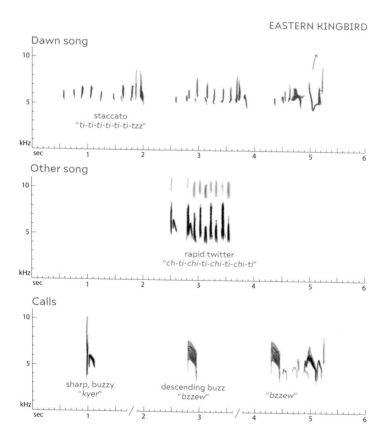

EASTERN KINGBIRD

Dawn song

staccato
"ti-ti-ti-ti-ti-ti-tzz"

Other song

rapid twitter
"ch-ti-chi-ti-chi-ti-chi-ti"

Calls

sharp, buzzy
"kyer"

descending buzz
"bzzew"

"bzzew"

EASTERN KINGBIRD

black crown and face

dark gray

black tail with
white tip

white chin and throat

red crown feathers of
adult usually concealed

Juvenile

male

female

note extent of notches
on outer
primaries vs female

EASTERN KINGBIRD

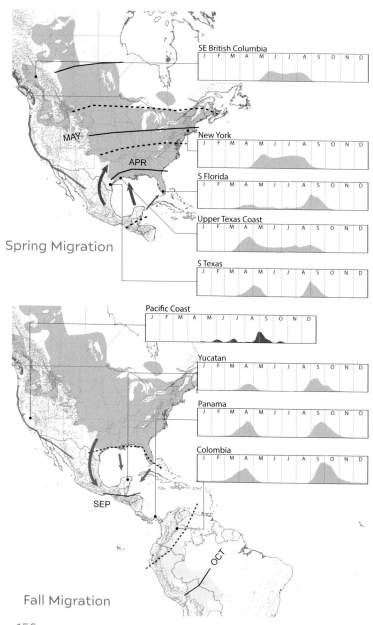

SE British Columbia
J F M A M J J A S O N D

New York
J F M A M J J A S O N D

S Florida
J F M A M J J A S O N D

Upper Texas Coast
J F M A M J J A S O N D

S Texas
J F M A M J J A S O N D

Spring Migration

MAY

APR

Pacific Coast
J F M A M J J A S O N D

Yucatan
J F M A M J J A S O N D

Panama
J F M A M J J A S O N D

Colombia
J F M A M J J A S O N D

SEP

OCT

Fall Migration

Gray Kingbird

Tyrannus dominicensis
L 9.2–9.4″ (23.3–23.9 cm), WT 1.3–1.8 oz (36.9–51.0 g)

GENERAL IDENTIFICATION Aptly named, the Gray Kingbird is the only kingbird in our region that has such pale overall coloration. It has a medium-gray crown and mantle, and dark gray to brown wings and tail. The underparts from chin to belly are white. Auriculars are dark gray, giving it a dusky mask. Gray's bill is longer and thicker than those of most of the common kingbirds in North America. Gray has concealed orange in its crown (lacking in juveniles). Its tail is proportionately long compared with the common kingbirds, and with its longer, heavier bill, structurally it resembles Tropical Kingbird, to which it is closely related. Its median coverts have whitish feather edges, giving the impression of a white upper wingbar. The tail is slightly notched, like that of Tropical. In flight, underwings are whitish to pale yellow. The juvenal plumage is like adult's except upperparts may be washed with light brown. Prebasic molt begins on summering grounds (body feathers) but completes (flight feathers) on wintering grounds.

VOCALIZATIONS Gray's song is a rapid series of short high-pitched notes, ending with an accelerated twitter, very much like that of Tropical. Calls and songs are superficially like Eastern Kingbird, but Gray's call notes are cleaner, lacking the buzzy tones in Eastern's calls and songs.

HABITAT, DISTRIBUTION, AND SEASONAL STATUS Gray Kingbird is found primarily along the coast. It can be found in open pine woodlands, open palmetto stands, and mangrove forests, often near water. Gray Kingbird can also be found in urban areas, often sitting on low powerlines. Its nest is an open bowl, loosely constructed of twigs and various plant fibers. The nest is generally exposed and placed at low to medium heights in various shrubs or medium-sized trees, such as mangroves, scrub oak, palmetto, acacia, and casuarina. The nests are often placed above water, but, in urban areas, can often be placed in high-traffic areas, such as in small trees around parking lots.

Gray Kingbird makes its home in the Caribbean. It is a year-round resident of Haiti, the Dominican Republic, and Puerto Rico. Its range expands during the summer breeding season to encompass Cuba, Bermuda, the Bahamas, coastal Florida, and Alabama. Birds arrive on their breeding grounds in mid-Mar. (Cuba) and late Mar. to early Apr. (Florida). During strong southeasterlies, some birds may overshoot as far west as the upper Texas coast and north along the Atlantic coast through South Carolina. It is an uncommon but regular migrant in coastal Yucatan, Quintana Roo, Belize, and along the Caribbean coast of Costa Rica. Breeding birds depart to wintering grounds in mid-Aug., with most gone by early Sept. Migratory birds winter in northern South America, arriving in mid-Aug. and staying through the end of Apr. Gray Kingbird is a rare but regular vagrant to the Atlantic coast, Great Lakes, and Midwest, with most records between Aug. and late Nov.

SIMILAR SPECIES Gray Kingbird is generally unmistakable. A pale or backlit Eastern Kingbird can superficially resemble Gray in plumage, but note Gray's larger size, bulkier bill, bulkier body, and longer tail compared with Eastern. Eastern's upperparts are solid black, not gray. Eastern also will not show contrasting dark auriculars. Eastern has white tail tips. Gray has short to intermediate primary projection. In flight, note Gray's whitish to pale yellow underwing (dark in Eastern). Songs and calls are similar, but Eastern's calls and songs often include short buzzy notes with a descending quality, while Gray's vocalizations do not include buzzy notes.

Songs and calls

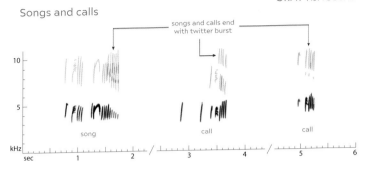

songs and calls end
with twitter burst

10

5

kHz

sec   1   2   3   4   5   6

song   call   call

GRAY KINGBIRD

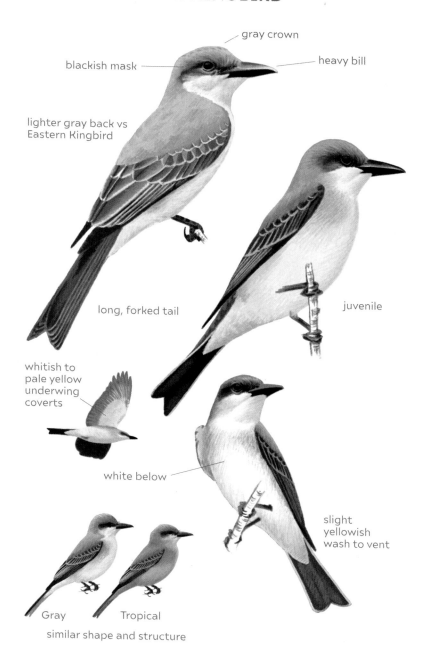

gray crown

blackish mask

heavy bill

lighter gray back vs
Eastern Kingbird

long, forked tail

juvenile

whitish to
pale yellow
underwing
coverts

white below

slight
yellowish
wash to vent

Gray   Tropical

similar shape and structure

GRAY KINGBIRD

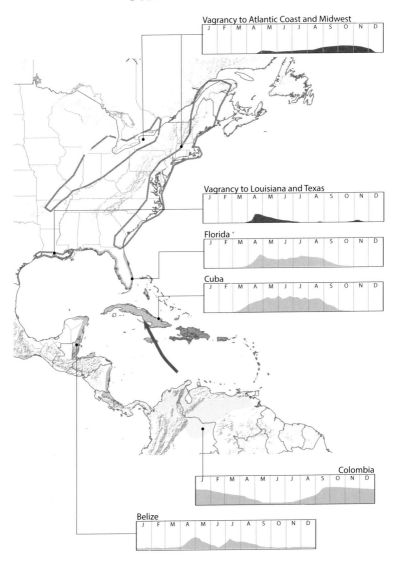

Vagrancy to Atlantic Coast and Midwest

J	F	M	A	M	J	J	A	S	O	N	D

Vagrancy to Louisiana and Texas

J	F	M	A	M	J	J	A	S	O	N	D

Florida

J	F	M	A	M	J	J	A	S	O	N	D

Cuba

J	F	M	A	M	J	J	A	S	O	N	D

Colombia

J	F	M	A	M	J	J	A	S	O	N	D

Belize

J	F	M	A	M	J	J	A	S	O	N	D

Loggerhead Kingbird

Tyrannus caudifasciatus

L 9.1–10.2″ (23.1–25.9 cm)

WT *T. c. bahamensis* 1.46–1.75 oz (41.3–49.5 g)
T. c. caudifasciatus 1.2–1.7 oz (34.0–48.2 g)

GENERAL IDENTIFICATION The Loggerhead Kingbird is a
large, black and white kingbird with a large bill. It is strictly a bird
of the Caribbean islands. Although it is largely non-migratory,
it occasionally wanders to south Florida. With its black crown,
dark gray mantle, blackish wings, black tail, and contrasting white
underparts, it recalls Eastern Kingbird. However, it has a very
short primary projection compared with Eastern (a long-distance
migrant). In flight, Loggerhead thus has more rounded wings than
Eastern. Eastern further differs in having a nearly black mantle,
unlike the dark gray mantle of Loggerhead. Loggerhead's tail is
square tipped, and the tip of the tail, depending on subspecies,
may be gray or white. There is significant subspecific variation
among the main islands of the Caribbean. In our region, the two
relevant subspecies are *T. c. bahamensis* from the Bahamas and
T. c. caudifasciatus from Cuba, both of which appear to have
wandered to Florida at times. Both subspecies are similar in overall
coloration, size, and structure, but there are subtle differences.
Subspecies *bahamensis* is overall slightly lighter in coloration than
caudifasciatus. Whereas *bahamensis* has a dark gray to black crown,
caudifasciatus has a black crown. The mantle of *bahamensis* is lighter
than that of *caudifasciatus* and often has an olive tint. The vent and
lower belly of *bahamensis* has a light wash of yellow whereas that
of *caudifasciatus* is white. The wing ground color of *bahamensis* is
brownish whereas that of *caudifasciatus* is dark gray to black. The tip
of the tail in *caudifasciatus* is white like Eastern Kingbird but gray in
bahamensis.

VOCALIZATIONS Loggerhead gives a variety of short call notes, twitters, and chatters. The vocalizations of *bahamensis* and *caudifasciatus* differ noticeably. The song of *caudifasciatus* is a series of very rapid hollow sounding metallic "*pik*" notes, somewhat like a rapid cowbird rattle or Ladder-backed Woodpecker (*Dryobytes scalaris*) whinny. *Tyrannus c. caudifasciatus* gives a squeaky call note, which, when given in rapid succession, sounds like a squeaky chatter; *caudifasciatus* also gives some low, burry or buzzy "*trdrrrrrrr*" calls. *Tyrannus c. bahamensis* gives a twitter like that of *caudifasciatus*, but its twitters have a less metallic tone than *caudifasciatus*. The twitters of *bahamensis* are often long and drawn out, increasing and decreasing in pitch. Call of *bahamensis* consists of burry notes at a higher frequency than that of *caudifasciatus*. Unlike *caudifasciatus*, *bahamensis* does not usually give squeaky calls. The twitters of *bahamensis* are often followed by short descending burry "*cheurr*" notes.

HABITAT, DISTRIBUTION, AND SEASONAL STATUS Unlike most other kingbirds, the Loggerhead Kingbird prefers to hunt from middle to high perches in wooded areas, including forests, mangrove stands, and lowland scrub. The Loggerhead Kingbird can also be found in garden-like settings and open woodlands in its normal range, especially in winter when the migratory Gray Kingbird vacates the region. Its nests are open bowls composed of twigs and placed in the fork of a horizontal branch at low to medium height.

Loggerhead Kingbird is a year-round resident of the Bahamas and the northern Caribbean islands from Cuba to Puerto Rico. It is resident but rare on Hispaniola. Except for local movements, it is largely non-migratory. However, it is a very rare vagrant to south Florida with records from the Florida Keys to the Miami region. So far, all records of vagrants have occurred between Dec. and May. Multiple subspecies across Caribbean islands may be designated species status in the future, so any vagrant should be carefully documented.

LOGGERHEAD KINGBIRD

black crown and face

long, heavy bill

olive-gray back

strongly peaked crown

large kingbird

bahamensis

yellowish vent

reduced pale tail tips vs Cuban ssp

caudifasciatus

pale tail tip and outer tail

distinctive shape in flight

rounded outer primaries

SIMILAR SPECIES Loggerhead Kingbird is most like Eastern Kingbird, but note Loggerhead's larger size, longer and larger bill, and short primary projection. Gray Kingbird is paler in plumage, has a dusky mask, and a slightly forked tail.

LOGGERHEAD KINGBIRD
caudifasciatus

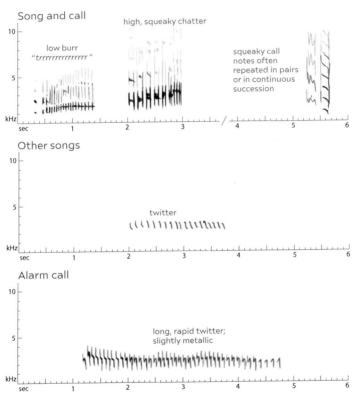

Song and call

high, squeaky chatter

low burr
"trrrrrrrrrrrrrrr"

squeaky call notes often repeated in pairs or in continuous succession

Other songs

twitter

Alarm call

long, rapid twitter; slightly metallic

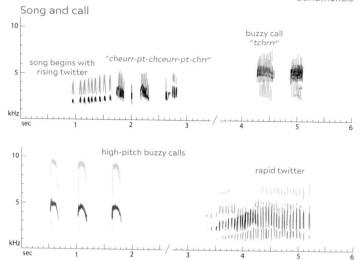

LOGGERHEAD KINGBIRD
bahamensis

Song and call

buzzy call
"tchrrr"

song begins with
rising twitter

"cheurr-pt-chceurr-pt-chrr"

high-pitch buzzy calls

rapid twitter

LOGGERHEAD KINGBIRD

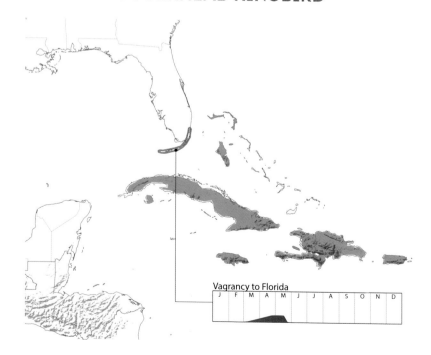

Vagrancy to Florida

J F M A M J J A S O N D

Scissor-tailed Flycatcher

Tyrannus forficatus

L both sexes without tail 4.3″ (10.9 cm)

♂ with tail 9.8–14.6″ (24.9–37.1 cm)

♀ with tail 8.7–11.8″ (22.1–30.0 cm)

WT ♂ 1.31–1.46 oz (37.1–41.3 g)

♀ 1.30–1.51 oz (36.9–42.8 g)

GENERAL IDENTIFICATION Despite its name and its long tail, the Scissor-tailed Flycatcher is a kingbird. Its closest relative is the Western Kingbird, with which it occasionally hybridizes. The adult male's long tail makes Scissor-tailed Flycatchers unmistakable. Tails of females are approximately 30% shorter, but still distinctly longer than those of other flycatchers and kingbirds. Scissor-tailed Flycatcher's head, mantle, throat, and chest are pale gray to white, contrasting with black wings and a light pink belly. The crown contains concealed orange feathers (lacking in juveniles). In flight, pinkish underwing coverts are sometimes conspicuous. The tail is black with extensive white in the outer-tail feathers. Tail is held stiff and straight. Birds undergoing molt may have shortened tails and may structurally look like kingbirds. The prebasic molt is primarily completed on breeding grounds or during temporary migratory stopovers (coastal Texas). Adult tail feathers can become extremely worn by July, with only the black parts of the tail feathers remaining (white parts eroded), but by early Aug. these worn tail feathers have been replaced with a fresh new set.

VOCALIZATIONS Song is a rapid staccato series of low-pitched, squeaky "*pip*" notes and a few "*pi-chur*" or "*prrp*" notes, accelerating and rising in pitch at the end of the song. It frequently gives single note "*pip*" calls and various chatters. Songs and calls can sometimes be remarkably like Western Kingbird's, but Western Kingbird's call notes tend to be higher pitched than Scissor-tailed Flycatcher.

HABITAT, DISTRIBUTION, AND SEASONAL STATUS Scissor-tailed Flycatchers are iconic summer residents of the Central Plains, because of their preference for open grasslands and prairies with scattered bushes and small trees. They can be found in agricultural areas and along country roads, often perched on fence lines and powerlines. Their nests are open bowls made of various plant fibers placed in the outer canopy of trees or tall structures like telephone poles.

Scissor-tailed Flycatchers breed from southern Texas/northeastern Mexico north to Kansas, and from western Texas east to western Louisiana and Missouri. Scissor-tailed winters from southern Mexico south to Panama. Spring migrants arrive in southern Texas in early Mar., spreading across the breeding range to the north by early Apr. Birds begin moving south in late Aug., with southbound migration peaking between late Sep. and mid-Oct. By Nov. most birds have vacated the United States, although small numbers may linger through the winter along the Texas coast. It is an uncommon but regular winter visitor in south Florida. Scissor-tailed Flycatchers are known to wander and, although rare, vagrants may turn up anywhere in the United States and southern Canada. Along the Pacific coast, vagrants are most often found in Sept. and Oct. Scissor-tailed is known to migrate (especially in fall) and winter in loose flocks.

SIMILAR SPECIES The Scissor-tailed Flycatcher is generally unmistakable. From a distance or in silhouette it may look like a Fork-tailed, but note the thinner and proportionately longer tail feathers of adult male Fork-tailed. Fork-tailed's tail is floppier and less straight than Scissor-tailed. Females, immatures, and birds undergoing molt can be confused with Western Kingbirds, but color patterns should be diagnostic.

SCISSOR-TAILED FLYCATCHER

juveniles shorter tailed with less color on flanks

wings dark with pale blue-gray edged feathers and exceedingly long tail

salmon wash to flanks and belly

females usually shorter tailed

juvenile

juvenile with whiter underwing coverts

adults

Call and Song

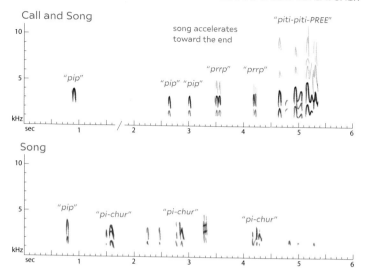

song accelerates
toward the end

"piti-piti-PREE"

"pip"

"pip" "pip"

"prrp"   "prrp"

Song

"pip"

"pi-chur"

"pi-chur"

"pi-chur"

SCISSOR-TAILED FLYCATCHER

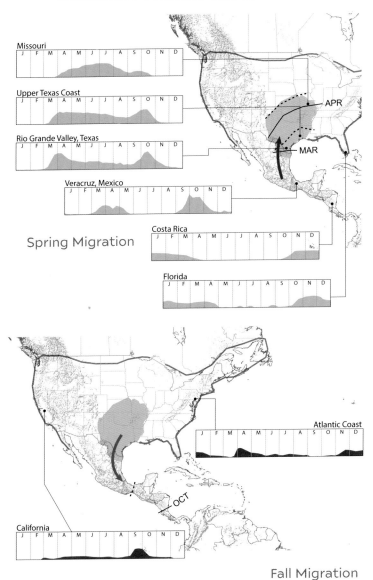

Missouri

Upper Texas Coast

Rio Grande Valley, Texas

Veracruz, Mexico

Costa Rica

Florida

Spring Migration

APR

MAR

Atlantic Coast

OCT

California

Fall Migration

Fork-tailed Flycatcher
Tyrannus savana

♂ L 14.6–15.9″ (37.0–40.5 cm), WT 1.10–1.19 oz (31.2–34.0 g)

♀ L 11.0–11.8″ (27.9–30.0 cm), WT 0.95–1.20 oz (26.9–34.0 g)

GENERAL IDENTIFICATION With its contrasting black-and-white pattern and long tail, Fork-tailed Flycatcher is usually unmistakable. Its black crown, face, wings, and tail contrast with the immaculate white chin, lower neck, breast, and belly. Fork-tailed has concealed yellow in its crown (lacking in juveniles). Although its tail is long like Scissor-tailed's, it has a proportionately smaller body, so the tail appears proportionately longer. Fork-tailed's tail is also more ribbon-like than Scissor-tailed's, which is stiff and straight. Collectively, these structural differences give Fork-tailed a more graceful and dainty look, like a small ball with long, thin streamers attached to it; the thin, long tail often flops in the wind. Its underwing coverts are white, whereas they are pink in Scissor-tailed and dark in Eastern Kingbird. Fork-tailed's flight is more undulating than that of kingbirds or Scissor-tailed.

Fork-tailed has four subspecies: non-migratory *T. s. monachus* (southern Mexico to Colombia); migratory *savana* (central and southern South America); *T. s. sanctaemartae* (northern Colombia and Venezuela); and *T. s. circumdatus* (northwestern Brazil). Vagrants to the United States are thought to be *savana* although *monachus* may also be possible. Subtle differences exist between subspecies. *Tyrannus s. monachus* and *T. s. sanctaemartae* have more complete white collars and pale gray backs that contrast with the black crown. *Tyrannus s. savana* has a more limited white collar and a darker gray back that shows only moderate contrast with the black crown. In adult males of all subspecies, outer primaries are deeply notched (no notching in female or juvenal flight feathers). *Tyrannus s. savana* shows deep notches in the outermost three primaries (p10 to p8). In *T. s. monachus*, notches are less deep, with only p10 and p9 being distinctly notched.

Adults undergo a complete prebasic molt on nonbreeding grounds, but because of the different migratory patterns of Northern and Southern Hemisphere birds, subspecies differ in their molt strategies. *Tyrannus s. monachus* primarily molts from July to Sept., appearing fresh from Sept. to Dec. and worn from Jan. to Aug. By contrast, the austral migrant *T. s. savana* molts from Apr. to July, appearing fresh from July to Nov. and worn from Dec. to May.

VOCALIZATIONS Fork-tailed Flycatcher's distinctive song consists of a long series of very rapid, insect-like twitters. Its call is a single-note, high-pitched "*tic*," which sounds more like a warbler's than the calls of other species of the genus *Tyrannus* do.

HABITAT, DISTRIBUTION, AND SEASONAL STATUS The Fork-tailed Flycatcher prefers open habitats, including savannas, grasslands, farmlands, and woodland edges. On breeding grounds, they prefer open areas with scattered trees for nesting. Nests are open bowls composed of twigs or grass and lined on the inside with soft plant fibers.

Fork-tailed is a year-round resident from southern Mexico to northern South America, including Colombia, Venezuela, and the lower Amazon in Brazil. The northern subspecies, *monachus* (Mexico to Colombia), is mostly non-migratory. The South American subspecies, *savana* (central South America), is highly migratory. During the southern summer, from late July to Feb., *savana* expands southwards across southern South America as far as central Argentina to breed. *Tyrannus s. sanctaemartae* (northern Colombia and Venezuela) may show similar migratory patterns as *savana*. Fork-tailed wanders widely and, although rare, it has been recorded in almost every state in the United States and in southern Canada. Most records, however, are from east of the Rocky Mountains. Vagrants to the Atlantic coast occur from spring through fall (Apr. to Dec.), with most being seen between late Aug. and early Dec. It is likely that most spring birds in the east pertain to the southern migratory subspecies *savana*, given that spring corresponds with the austral fall migration period. Fork-tailed is generally absent from the Atlantic coast in winter. Vagrants to the Gulf of Mexico coast, from Texas to Florida, have been recorded in every month of the year, including in the winter. Some of these wintering Gulf Coast birds may be of the more proximal *monachus* subspecies, but more study is needed to confirm this. Vagrants have been recorded west of the Rockies (with records from Alberta, Idaho, Washington, Nevada, and California), but at much lower frequencies than in the east. Records from western United States are overwhelmingly fall birds and are probably of *monachus*.

SIMILAR SPECIES Fork-tailed Flycatcher is structurally like Scissor-tailed, but note proportionately smaller body and longer tail, different plumage patterns, and thinner and floppier tail. On distant birds, Fork-tailed Flycatcher may recall Eastern Kingbird because its thin tail can be difficult to see, and many vagrants to the United States are in molt and may therefore show much reduced tail length, adding to confusion. However, Fork-tailed Flycatcher has a smaller body than Eastern Kingbird and has a contrasting gray back compared with Eastern Kingbird. Fork-tailed's secondaries and wing coverts lack pale edges, giving a more uniform black wing. Eastern Kingbird has bold white edges to its secondaries and pale edges to its wing covert feathers. Pin-tailed Whydah (*Vidua macroura*) may be superficially like Fork-tailed, but confusion is unlikely when seen well.

FORK-TAILED FLYCATCHER

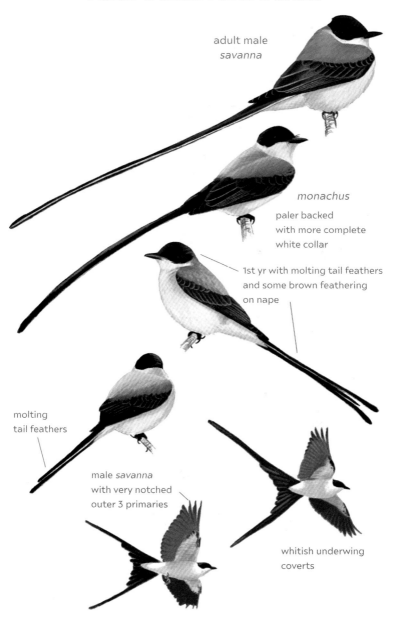

adult male
savanna

monachus
paler backed
with more complete
white collar

1st yr with molting tail feathers
and some brown feathering
on nape

molting
tail feathers

male *savanna*
with very notched
outer 3 primaries

whitish underwing
coverts

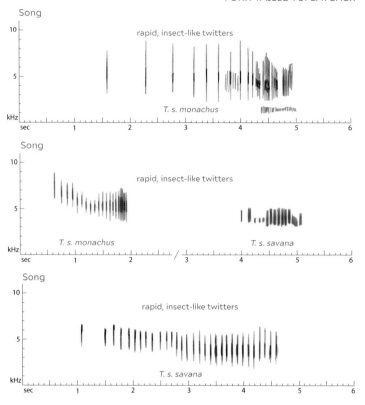

Song

rapid, insect-like twitters

T. s. monachus

Song

rapid, insect-like twitters

T. s. monachus

T. s. savana

Song

rapid, insect-like twitters

T. s. savana

FORK-TAILED FLYCATCHER

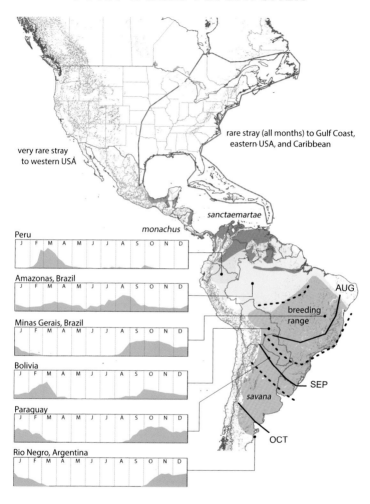

rare stray (all months) to Gulf Coast, eastern USA, and Caribbean

very rare stray to western USA

sanctaemartae

monachus

Peru

Amazonas, Brazil

Minas Gerais, Brazil

Bolivia

Paraguay

Rio Negro, Argentina

AUG

breeding range

SEP

savana

OCT

FORK-TAILED FLYCATCHER VAGRANCY

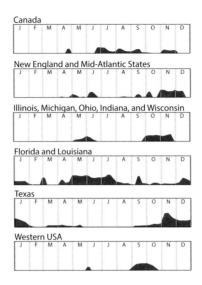

Canada

J	F	M	A	M	J	J	A	S	O	N	D

New England and Mid-Atlantic States

J	F	M	A	M	J	J	A	S	O	N	D

Illinois, Michigan, Ohio, Indiana, and Wisconsin

J	F	M	A	M	J	J	A	S	O	N	D

Florida and Louisiana

J	F	M	A	M	J	J	A	S	O	N	D

Texas

J	F	M	A	M	J	J	A	S	O	N	D

Western USA

J	F	M	A	M	J	J	A	S	O	N	D

Kingbird Hybrids

Members of the flycatcher family tend not to hybridize frequently, and when they do, the offspring are not viable. The chart showing kingbird hybrids shows all reported hybrids, color-coded by their frequency of occurrence (dark squares indicate frequent occurrence, pale squares infrequent). The hybrids in this chart are ordered according to the most recent phylogeny of kingbird species as discussed in the Introduction. The three most common hybrids, although still very rare, are Western × Eastern Kingbird, Western Kingbird × Scissor-tailed Flycatcher, and Tropical × Gray Kingbird. It can be seen from this diagram that the most common hybrids involve closely related species, especially if their ranges overlap. Western Kingbird × Scissor-tailed Flycatcher and Western × Eastern Kingbird hybrids are the most likely in our region. Tropical × Gray Kingbird hybrids have been reported in Florida. We note that hybridization between closely related Eastern and Cassin's Kingbirds has been reported, but because their ranges barely overlap, such hybrids are very rare despite the genetic similarity of the two species.

We illustrate below the three hybrids most likely to be seen. Western × Eastern Kingbird hybrids, as expected, look like a blend between the two species: a kingbird with grayish upperparts and whitish underparts with a pale wash of yellow on the belly. Such birds often have a pale tip to the tail, reminiscent of the white tail tip of Eastern Kingbird, but duller. Western × Eastern Kingbirds may be superficially similar in color to Gray Kingbird, but note that Gray Kingbird has a longer and heavier bill and shorter primary projection. Western Kingbird × Scissor-tailed Flycatcher hybrid looks like a Scissor-tailed Flycatcher with a shorter tail and pale yellow underparts, as opposed to the pinkish coloration of Scissor-tailed. These hybrids may also have a slightly greenish tint to the mantle. Tropical × Gray Kingbird does not look unusual structurally given the very similar sizes and structures of the two species. Hybrids of these two species tend to look like pale Gray Kingbirds with a yellow wash on the lower belly and vent.

Couch's Kingbird × Scissor-tailed Flycatcher hybrids have been reported, but these are exceedingly rare, and some reported hybrids may have been juvenile Western Kingbirds in the process of molting, resulting in a deep fork to the tail. Hybrids between Couch's and Tropical Kingbirds have been reported, but given the difficulty in separating these two species, there is little hope that one can identify a hybrid visually. Loggerhead × Gray Kingbird hybrids have been reported but are unlikely to occur in our area. When studying a possible hybrid, we recommend obtaining recordings of vocalizations.

KINGBIRD HYBRIDS

HYBRIDS

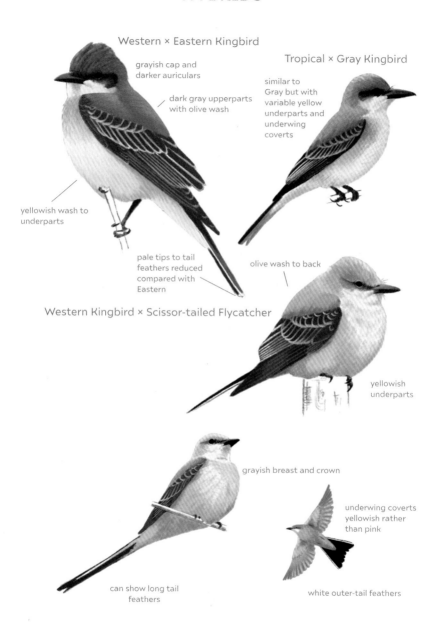

Western × Eastern Kingbird

grayish cap and darker auriculars

dark gray upperparts with olive wash

Tropical × Gray Kingbird

similar to Gray but with variable yellow underparts and underwing coverts

yellowish wash to underparts

pale tips to tail feathers reduced compared with Eastern

olive wash to back

Western Kingbird × Scissor-tailed Flycatcher

yellowish underparts

grayish breast and crown

underwing coverts yellowish rather than pink

can show long tail feathers

white outer-tail feathers

Bibliography

Alderfer, J., and Dunn, J., 2017, National Geographic Field Guide to the Birds of North America, 7th ed., *National Geographic Society*, Washington, DC, 592.

Bent, A. C., 1963, *Life Histories of North American Flycatchers, Larks, Swallows, and Their Allies*, US National Museum Bulletin 179.

Bowers, R. K., Jr. and Dunning, J. B., Jr., 1987, Nutting's Flycatcher (*Myiarchus nuttingi*) from Arizona, *American Birds*, 41(1): 5–10.

Brush, T., 2020, Couch's Kingbird (*Tyrannus couchii*), version 1.0, Birds of the World (A. F. Poole and F. B. Gill, Editors), Cornell Lab of Ornithology, Ithaca, NY, USA. https://doi.org/10.2173/bow.coukin.01

Calvert, K. B. and Welch, M. J., 2015, First record of Couch's Kingbird, *Tyrannus couchii*, in Maryland. *Maryland Birdlife*, 64(2): 2–6.

Cardiff, S. W., and Dittmann, D. L., 2000, Brown-crested Flycatcher (*Myiarchus tyrannulus*), in *The Birds of North America*, no. 496 (A. Poole and F. Gill, Editors.), *Birds of North America, Inc.*, Philadelphia.

Cardiff, S. W., and Dittmann, D. L., 2020, Ash-throated Flycatcher (*Myiarchus cinerascens*), version 1.0. Birds of the World (A. F. Poole and F. B. Gill, Editors), Cornell Lab of Ornithology, Ithaca, NY, USA. https://doi.org/10.2173/bow. astfly.01

Dittmann, D. L. and Cardiff, S. W, 2000, Let's take another look: *Myiarchus* Flycatchers. *Louisiana Ornithological News*: 3–10.

Gamble, L. R., and Bergin, T. M., 2020, Western Kingbird (*Tyrannus verticalis*), version 1.0. Birds of the World (A. F. Poole, Editor), Cornell Lab of Ornithology, Ithaca, NY, USA. https://doi.org/10.2173/bow.weskin.01

Harvey, M. G., Bravo, G. A., Claramunt, S., Cuervo, A. M., Derryberry, G. E., Battilana, J., Seeholzer, G. F., McKay, J. S., O'Meara, B. C., Faircloth, B. C., and Edwards, S. V., 2020, The evolution of a tropical biodiversity hotspot. *Science* 370:1343–1348.

Howell, S. N. G, 2010, *Molt in North American Birds. Houghton Mifflin Harcourt*, New York, 267.

Howell, S. N., Lewington, I., and Russell, W., 2014, *Rare Birds of North America. Princeton University Press*, Princeton, NJ, 428.

Jahn, A. E., and Tuero, D. T., 2020, Fork-tailed Flycatcher (*Tyrannus savana*), version 1.0. Birds of the World (T. S. Schulenberg, Editor), Cornell Lab of Ornithology, Ithaca, NY, USA. https://doi.org/10.2173/bow.fotfly.01

Joseph, L., 2020, La Sagra's Flycatcher (*Myiarchus sagrae*), version 1.0. Birds of the World (J. del Hoyo, A. Elliott, J. Sargatal, D. A. Christie, and E. de Juana, Editors), Cornell Lab of Ornithology, Ithaca, NY, USA. https://doi.org/10.2173/bow. lasfly.01

Joseph, L., 2020, Nutting's Flycatcher (*Myiarchus nuttingi*), version 1.0. Birds of the World (J. del Hoyo, A. Elliott, J. Sargatal, D. A. Christie, and E. de Juana, Editors), Cornell Lab of Ornithology, Ithaca, NY, USA. https://doi.org/10.2173/bow. nutfly.01

Kaufman, K., 1990, *A Field Guide to Advanced Birding: Birding Challenges and How to Approach Them. Houghton Mifflin*, Boston .

Lee, C. T., 2022, Field identification of Tropical and Couch's Kingbirds, *Texas Birds Annual* 18: 7–19.

Lee, C. T., and Birch, A., 2023, *Field Guide to North American Flycatchers: Empidonax and Pewees, Princeton University Press*, Princeton, NJ, 157.

Lee, C. T., Birch, A., and Eubanks, T. L., 2008, Field identification of Western and Eastern Wood-pewees. *Birding*, 40(4): 34–40.

Lowther, P. E., Pyle, P., and Patten, M. A., 2020, Thick-billed Kingbird (*Tyrannus crassirostris*), version 1.0. Birds of the World (P. G. Rodewald, Editor), Cornell Lab of Ornithology, Ithaca, NY, USA. https://doi.org/10.2173/bow.thbkin.01

McCarthy, E. M., 2006, *Handbook of Avian Hybrids of the World. Oxford University Press*, Oxford, 583.

McCaskie, G. and Patten, M. A., 1994, Status of the Fork-tailed Flycatcher (*Tyrannus savana*) in the United States and Canada, *Western Birds*, 25: 113–127.

McGowan, K. J. and Spahn, R., 2004, A probable Couch's Kingbird × Scissor-tailed Flycatcher in Livingston Co., New York, *The Kingbird*, 54(1): 2–12.

Miller, K. E., and Lanyon, W. E., 2020, Great Crested Flycatcher (*Myiarchus crinitus*), version 1.0. Birds of the World (A. F. Poole, Editor), Cornell Lab of Ornithology, Ithaca, NY, USA. https://doi.org/10.2173/bow.grcfly.01

Mobley, J. A., and de Juana, E., 2020, Loggerhead Kingbird (*Tyrannus caudifasciatus*), version 1.0. Birds of the World (J. del Hoyo, A. Elliott, J. Sargatal, D. A. Christie, and E. de Juana, Editors), Cornell Lab of Ornithology, Ithaca, NY, USA, https://doi.org/10.2173/bow.logkin.01

Murphy, M. T. and Pyle, P., 2020, Eastern Kingbird (*Tyrannus tyrannus*), version 1.0. Birds of the World (P. G. Rodewald, Editor), Cornell Lab of Ornithology, Ithaca, NY, USA. https://doi.org/10.2173/bow.easkin.01

Pieplow, N., 2019, *Peterson Field Guide to Bird Sounds of Western North America*, Peterson Field Guides. *Houghton Mifflin Harcourt*, Boston.

Pranty, B., Kratter, A. W., and Ponzo, V., 2016, Status and distribution in Florida of Tropical Kingbird (*Tyrannus melancholicus*) and Couch's Kingbird (*Tyrannus couchii*), *Florida Field Naturalist*, 44(3): 83–105.

Pyle, P., 2022, *Identification Guide to North American Birds*, part 1, 2nd ed. *Slate Creek Press*, Forest Knolls, CA, 697.

Regosin, J. V., 2020, Scissor-tailed Flycatcher (*Tyrannus forficatus*), version 1.0. Birds of the World (A. F. Poole, Editor), Cornell Lab of Ornithology, Ithaca, NY, USA. https://doi.org/10.2173/bow.sctfly.01

Rowland, F., 2009, Identifying *Empidonax* flycatchers, the ratio approach, *Birding*, 41: 30–38.

Sibley, D. A., 2014, *The Sibley Guide to Birds. Knopf*, New York, 624.

Smith, G. A., and Jackson, J. A., 2020, Gray Kingbird (*Tyrannus dominicensis*), version 1.0. Birds of the World (A. F. Poole and F. B. Gill, Editors), Cornell Lab of Ornithology, Ithaca, NY, USA. https://doi.org/10.2173/bow.grykin.01

Stouffer, P. C., Chesser, R. T. and Jahn, A. E., 2020, Tropical Kingbird (*Tyrannus melancholicus*), version 1.0. Birds of the World (S. M. Billerman, Editor), Cornell Lab of Ornithology, Ithaca, NY, USA. https://doi.org/10.2173/bow.trokin.01

Tweit, R. C., and Tweit, J. C., 2020, Cassin's Kingbird (*Tyrannus vociferans*), version 1.0. Birds of the World (A. F. Poole and F. B. Gill, Editors), Cornell Lab of Ornithology, Ithaca, NY, USA. https://doi.org/10.2173/bow.caskin.01

Tweit, R. C., and Tweit, J. C., 2020, Dusky-capped Flycatcher (*Myiarchus tuberculifer*), version 1.0. Birds of the World (A. F. Poole and F. B. Gill, Editors), Cornell Lab of Ornithology, Ithaca, NY, USA. https://doi.org/10.2173/bow.ducfly.01

Yunick, R. P., 2008, An examination of wing tip shape to identify male and female Eastern Kingbirds, *North American Bird Bander*, 33(1): 7–12.

Useful Websites

Birds of the World by the Cornell Laboratory of Ornithology—detailed description of the natural history of the birds of the world (birdsoftheworld.org)

Macaulay Library for bird information and resources including bird sounds (macaulaylibrary.org)

xeno-canto—a collection of wildlife sounds from around the world, including birds (xeno-canto.org)

Peterson Field Guide to Bird Sounds by Nathan Pieplow (academy.allaboutbirds.org/peterson-field-guide-to-bird-sounds)

Surfbirds—a website archive of advanced identification articles, trip reports, and photographs, along with updates to all volumes of the current *Field Guide to Flycatchers of North America* (surfbirds.com)

Index